THAT RASCAL MIND

Cheryl Wilfong

2010

Cheryl Wilfong
Heart Path Press, L3C
P.O. Box 336
Putney VT 05346
www.meditativegardener.com

©2011 Cheryl Wilfong

All rights reserved. No part of this book may be reproduced in any form or by any means, electronic or mechanical, including photocopying, recording, or by any information storage and retrieval system, without permission in writing from the publisher.

ISBN: 978-0-98256641-1

December 2010

Greetings Friends,

I continue to attend a writing group every week, so I'd like to share with you the best of my writing from 2010. My writing group facilitator, Jan Frazier, is Awake. She has seen through the machinations of the mind, and only uses the mind when she needs to. She lives in Awareness with the effervescence of causeless joy. As I receive the consistent nourishment of her teachings, I find my own writing drifting away from memoirs (except for that character Bill!) and toward incorporating my fascination with that rascal mind.

Since I'm writing an almost daily blog at www.themeditativegardener.blogspot.com, this year's essays include the Best of the Blog.

As usual, the Warning Label reads:

You may think you know the characters in these stories. But if you ask the people with those names about these incidents, you'll hear an entirely different story.

Appreciation to Mike Fleming for deep and quick editing. Gratitude to Carolyn Kasper for designing this book as well as *The Meditative Gardener* and *The Meditative Gardener Notebook*.

Thanks to you for reading,

CONTENTS

Waking Up   1

Red
The Woods Glow Red   5
A Hot Summer Day   6
It Takes a Village   7

Vintage Cheryl
Never Married   13
Second Languages   16
A Woman's Body Hair   19
Books and More Books   20

Travels
Our Pet Nene   27
Supai   30
British Soup   35
Far North   37
On Vacation—Again   40

Bill
Myrtle   45
Siddie's Eightieth Birthday   48

Flirters	51
Trapping	53

Best of the Blog
57

The Mind

Tranquility	93
The Reactive Mind	95
What I Would Have Liked to Have Said	97
My Favorite Word	99
Brain waves and Body Waves	101
What I Know Best	104
Skeleton	105

Darkness

The House on the Moors	111
The Name of the Dark	113

Tornado

Tornado Season	117

WAKING UP

A FEW YEARS ago I made the commitment to get up when I wake up. Often this means 4:00 A.M.

I used to read myself back to sleep, but the person who shares my bed complained that the light woke him up. I covered the lampshade with a towel to prevent the light diffusing into the room. Then he complained about the noise of pages turning.

He himself gets up when he wakes at midnight or 2:00 A.M. and goes downstairs to watch TV as his soporific.

If my goal is not sleep, but awakening, then, I rationalize, I should take advantage of my somewhat regular 4:00 A.M. wake up. After all, what if my spirit guides are waking me up? And I have to admit that knotty issues sometimes disentangle themselves with a flash of insight at 4:00 A.M., which may go to show that "sleeping on it" really works.

Oh-dark-thirty does have some advantages. It's a solitary time, perfect for the solitude I crave. In daylight hours, I have been known to ignore my sweetie when he is talking in order to focus on the computer. He does not appreciate that.

At four in the morning, I don't have to relate to anyone. I can read my Dharma lesson for the day, meditate for as long as I wish, write in my journal, and watch a new day being born.

RED

THE WOODS GLOW RED

Late in September, the evening's setting sun shines through gray drizzle, turning the sky a golden peach and giving the impression that everything is bathed in warm light. All of a sudden, our red maple has the reddest leaves—red, green, gold—all in a single branch. The stems of each leaf pulsate crimson.

Red light surrounds me. Oh! The small-leaf rhododendron! This afternoon I thought the inner leaves were yellowing, preparing to fall off, but this evening they are ruby red.

The trim on my house is magenta. When I give directions, I say "the house wearing lipstick." Tonight the color is deep and sensuous. Bill, who is color-blind, can't take his eyes off it.

As I drive out the driveway, the leaf cover in the woods glows deep pink. In front of the car, the headlights show washed-out yellow-tan dead leaves, but I look out my side window to see the secretly rosy hue of the leaf cover on the forest floor. The ground glows. Perhaps this is their natural color when human eyes aren't looking, aren't pinning things down as objects or as concepts?

This rosy red is what leaves would look like on Jupiter or Mars. The red pulse of life running through everything, dancing in the woods, sparking the trees to light up their leaves. Life, life, life.

A HOT SUMMER DAY

On a hot summer day, when the temperature and the humidity are equal numbers, when sweat rolls down my temples and trickles out of my armpits even though I'm sitting still, even though I'm totally naked, I clatter away on the computer keyboard until I have to submit to the heat, send my letter of resignation to the tropics. How do they do it down there near the equator?

I melt down the stairs to the kitchen, open the refrigerator door, and pull out a pitcher of watermelon juice. This is the season when I buy two quarter-sections of watermelon every day at Walker's farm stand, carve the red fruit into chunks, and run the flesh through the food processor, then pour it into a pitcher. This is the season when I drink half a watermelon a day in hopes that the gulping inflow will equal the dripping outflow.

Thus sustained, I slither down to the daylight basement where Bill has his music studio. Below ground it's 68 degrees. The 30-degree difference in descending eight feet feels sublime. Energy returns to life. I'm staying here in the embrace of Mother Earth, allowing her cool hand to rest on my hot forehead until my inner thermostat has readjusted, until I am revived and revivified.

IT TAKES A VILLAGE

My neighbor Connie said she needed three new rugs, so the next time I went to Ocean State Job Lots, I looked at rugs and bought one for her.

First of all, it was red—her favorite color. Second, it was five-by-seven, one of the sizes she was looking for. Third, it had random waves in the cinnamon color of her living room and bedroom walls. Fourth, Connie never goes shopping if she can possibly avoid it. Fifth, the price was right. I bought it. She liked it, and she put it on the linoleum in front of her washer and dryer.

A year later, our neighbor Lynn redid her living room for the first time in 30 years. When Connie and I met at Lynn's for morning meditation, we saw that Lynn had replaced a wall-hanging of a giraffe with a piece of red fabric with cinnamon circles.

"Connie," I said. "I think Lynn needs your rug."

Lynn put the rug in front of her brown sofa. It looks great.

Just goes to show you that it takes a village to decorate a home—at least on Partridge Road, where I live.

The first Sunday morning in January, I was backing out of Connie's driveway and being a little careless. I felt my Prius slip off the side of the road, downhill into a snowbank. I tried reversing and forwarding very quickly, but the anti-skid safety device stops the wheels from moving the instant they slip—not good for extracting oneself from slippery places.

I was just going to give up, walk home, and drive my truck down to pull myself out with a tow rope, but as I emerged from the car, here came two neighbors with their snow shovels. Theo is eight, and Lulu is six. Their snow shovels were quite small, but their intention was large. Ten minutes later, the snowbound tires were visible, and Theo, in his red snowsuit, was giving me advice about what to do next.

Connie brought her special metal strips that she carries in her car all winter, and she placed them behind my front tires. "Now straighten your steering wheel and back straight out."

The car moved, I turned the wheel, and found myself well and truly stuck in the snowbank, with the driver's side of the car pitching downhill.

"I'll drive you up to get your truck," Connie said.

Five minutes later, Theo was lying under the silver truck attaching the tow rope, then checking where to attach it to the blue car.

"Stand way back," I said to him and his sister, "just in case the tow rope snaps."

I got in my car; Connie drove the truck. The car moved slightly, angling more steeply downhill. We stopped.

Theo shook his head. "I think your car could tip over," he said. "We should have attached the tow rope to the downhill side of your car."

I looked at him. He was right. How does an eight-year-old know these things?

The next morning, I called AAA and ordered a wrecker. "Can you see your car from where you are?" the AAA woman asked.

"No," I said, "but I can be there in two minutes when he calls."

I picked up Lynn so we could go meditate at Connie's house, and from there I could see my car.

Ten minutes into the silence, my cell phone rang. I didn't answer, but tiptoed out of the living room to put on my boots and coat. By the time I walked out the door, the wrecker was maneuvering itself into position. Ten minutes after that, my Prius was out of the snowbank.

Lynn was finished with meditation and walked down to survey the site. "I'll drive your car to your house," she said, "while you drive your truck."

I tell you. It takes a village to rescue a car from a snow bank.

VINTAGE CHERYL

NEVER MARRIED

I'VE NEVER MARRIED, because no one has ever asked. Nor have I asked anyone to marry me.

I did ask my first boyfriend, Angelo, if I could come to Florida to live with him. "Sure," he said. At age 22, we were both virgins, and we didn't know what we were doing. Angelo was sweet and caring, but was a conservative second-generation Greek who believed in traditional roles. I kept my mouth shut for three months, and then departed—on good terms—to become a VISTA volunteer.

A year later, I followed my second boyfriend, Rod, to his home state of Hawai'i. I dreamed of having golden children with him, but his Japanese-American parents believed in racial purity, and my father had killed Japanese soldiers in the South Pacific during World War II. Of course, our parting seemed personal at the time—he didn't want a *haole* woman in his future, and I didn't want someone who was so focused on earning a lot of money—but greater forces were arrayed against us.

Fast-forward 12 years to Harlan, four days older than me and my emotional twin, my soulmate. I imagined our wedding in great detail while we were on a three-day meditation retreat together, but he broke up with me six months later, saying, "You're so much like me. I hate you." While I pleaded, "You're so much like me. I love you."

That's when I soured on the idea of soulmates. I hoped never to meet another one.

Four years later, on the Brattleboro Common, I saw this trim guy ride up on his yellow bicycle to the booth where I was volunteering. "Hi, I'm Bill," he said. "I have the next volunteer shift."

Mmmm, I thought.

Then a passerby stopped to talk to him, and I overheard Bill mention ". . . my estranged wife."

My one-minute-old fantasy died in its tracks. I was almost 41 and I knew that the life expectancy of rebound relationships was short. But this Bill and I sat and talked for an hour, then a little more. Before we parted, he asked me out on four dates.

It took Bill two and a half years for his divorce to become final and less time for him to have a vasectomy. With no children in our future, why get married? I certainly didn't want to mix my checkbook up with his. I was an accountant; he kept misplacing his wallet and losing his credit card. I owned my own house; he was about to lose the only asset he had—half-interest in a ranch house in Putney. I never could figure out why I would willingly give him half-interest in *my* house. Because of love? That just didn't make sense to me.

Three years later, on February 29, 1992—Leap Day—I did think about asking Bill to marry me, but the idea gave me such a severe anxiety attack that I couldn't bring myself to do it. The following Christmas he gave me a beautiful tanzanite and diamond ring that he and my sister had designed, made by the gemologist she worked for. It was the first ring that any boy or man had given me in my entire life. I broke into tears.

In 2003, while rafting the Colorado River in the Grand Canyon, Bill and I sauntered up Havasu Creek, dipping ourselves in the blue-green water and sunning ourselves on rocks under the watchful eyes of the mountain goats browsing nearby. We walked under a natural arbor spanning our path and turned to look at each other. There was where we married each other, under a blue sky heaven, sanctioned only by ourselves.

SECOND LANGUAGES

October 12 is the birthday of my first lover—Angelo Antoniou. The only son of Greek immigrant parents, he was bilingual, of course. The first bilingual person I had ever known.

Unless you count Gabby. Gabriel Garza helped Dad build the house I grew up in. I was just learning to speak English myself, but I did notice that skinny little Gabby talked funny. He and his wife Rita lived in a little green trailer on U.S. 40 in Greenfield. Rita was fat, and they didn't have children. That seemed strange. All adults had children. Well, all adults who were married. Everyone except Uncle Floyd and Aunt Hallie. They couldn't have children. So maybe Gabby and Rita couldn't have children either.

Then Gabby and Rita disappeared from our lives. And their green house trailer disappeared too, to be replaced by the Liberty Motel, where 20 years later I took my final liberty with Angelo's body. We made love for the last time on December 22, 1970, and then he disappeared from my life. A month later, he wrote me a letter saying he was getting married. That was good, because I was in love with Rod, and I followed him to Hawai'i six months later.

Rod Mitsuo spoke only a few words of Japanese because he was third-generation, but he understood his parents when they spoke Japanese to Rod's grandmother, who didn't seem to speak English. She wore wooden flip-flops that clacked on the floor, and she wore socks that were like mittens with a "thumb" for the big toe, so that the thong of the flip-flop could fit between the big toe and the second toe. Rod and his parents spoke Hawaiian-accented English, as well as the Hawaiian dialect of English called "pidgin."

Rod taught me various Japanese words: *shoyu, sushi, sashimi,* and how to count to three—*ichi, ni, san.* He was sansei—third-generation, his parents were nisei—second-generation. And he took me to Japanese samurai movies in Honolulu, where my favorite character was the blind woman samurai, Oichi.

Leaving Hawai'i, I went to a master's degree program in Vermont to be trained for an international career. Boyfriend #3, Joel, spoke French fluently because he'd been a Peace Corps volunteer in Senegal. He also spoke Wolof.

I left campus for my internship in Guatemala and met lover #4, Chris, who was bilingual in Spanish because he'd grown up in Guatemala. He also spoke beautiful Cakchiquel, the local Mayan dialect in Chimaltenango, where I was evaluating land-distribution programs for a community-development organization.

One-night-stand Mike was a sweet Peace Corps volunteer in the remote village of Chipiacul in Guatemala, so he spoke Spanish fluently. Meanwhile my own Spanish poked along in the present tense, with frequent work-arounds for words I didn't know.

I returned to the U.S. and fell into a depression that crushed my dream of living abroad. When I was a teenager, I had wanted to speak lots of languages, but now I realized that the closest I ever got was loving men who were fluent in another language.

Maybe Gabby started it all as he muttered to himself in Spanish while he stuccoed the walls of the three bedrooms of our house. After sleeping inside those Spanish-accented walls for 18 years, my sister and youngest brother and I each tried specializing in a language—German, Russian, and Spanish. But none of us became fluent.

Three days before he died, Dad called Gabby and asked him to come visit him. But Gabby was too decrepit and too slow. So, five days later, his son brought him to the funeral home instead.

A WOMAN'S BODY HAIR

Pluck her eyebrows.
Curl her eyelashes;
mascara them top and bottom.
Bleach her mustache.
Electrolyze her chin hairs.
Shave her underarms.
Wax her pubic hairs
along the bikini line.
Shave her legs often.

The hair on a woman's body must be managed
and disappeared,
so that she seems to be
as hairless as a young girl.
Woman
pretending to be pre-adolescent,
attractive to men.

Hairy men feel strong
over the body
of a hairless
child-
looking woman.

BOOKS AND
MORE BOOKS

"Look, Jane. Look."

"See Spot run."

Deciphering words was so much fun and so easy too. I read ahead to the end of the blue primer. Already I was hungry for more. More words. More stories.

As soon as I could, I read through the first six volumes of *Childcraft*. Then the ten volumes of *Uncle Arthur's Bible Stories*—twice. There wasn't that much to read at our house, so in sixth grade I began ordering books from Scholastic Book Service, which were offered once a month in the *Weekly Reader*. I'd spend an evening figuring how many books I could order for a dollar—one 25-cent book and two 35-cent books? Or four 25-cent books? I would wolf down the three or four books in short order and wonder if I could afford $1.25 next month.

My sister collected horses, but by the time I was a freshman in high school, I had to double-layer my little three-shelf bookcase. Much later, when I moved all my stuff out of my parents' house to my new house in Vermont, I had 24 boxes of paperback books. My brother, Paul, helped me load them into my 1972 Chevy Nova and said, "I never even read a book until I was 24." Apparently he was quite content with our two-bookshelf house. One bookshelf for Dad's thick volumes on standard-bred horse pedigrees. One shelf for Collier's encyclopedia. It was all just furniture to Paul.

I kept collecting books until I had an eight-foot wall totally filled with books from top to bottom—a shelf of Native American books, a shelf of Jungian books, a shelf of gardening books.

What do shelves and shelves of books say about their owner anyway? *Here is a knowledgeable person, a smart person, a well-read person. She has all this information at her fingertips.*

But a few years after I was introduced to Google, I realized I didn't need to have information at my fingertips, because Google can find it all and can get to it a *lot* faster. I was never going to read those hundreds of books again. Why was I keeping them?

I began to give books away. I still thought I had a precious collection. I gave the dozens of Jungian books to a Jungian group. I gave the Alice Bailey books together as a set. I began giving novels away as soon as I read them.

After all this thinning out, I have eight shelves of keepers. My main bookshelf is filled with unread books. Every three or four months, I take a bag of books to the Putney Library. A couple of times a year, I send a box of books to the Reader-to-Reader program. I don't go to the Windham County Reads book sale on Thanksgiving. I don't want any more books cluttering up my life.

What is reading anyway? For me, it's an escape, a way to get away from now.

I no longer spend summer afternoons or winter afternoons reading on the sofa. I read for 15 or 20 minutes before I go to sleep. Now, reading a novel feels like a luxury. When I go camping with my neighbors, I take a book a day to read. When I go on vacation, I take at least five books. Those and the travel books are what make up most of the weight in my suitcase.

In the Information Age, where we suffer from an avalanche of information, I've stopped listening to the news, reading magazines, or reading the newspaper. I used to collect all the newsletters that came in the mail and put them in my daypack to read on the airplane. But I can't possibly keep up with all the reading that comes every day in the mail or via e-mail, so I just give up. Now I just throw the newsletters away the day they arrive in my mailbox and try to be a good citizen even as I read less and less.

For several years, I kept lists of the books I had read that year, as if the list would somehow give meaning to my life. Then I realized that I don't remember books or their stories. I've read a few thousand books. So what? All this knowledge floats away sooner or later, usually sooner, but some small bits float away later.

So why do I read? To entertain myself? To procrastinate? To cocoon? To not notice what's going on in my life? It is my love of reading that has brought me so far—two master's degrees and authorship of two books. Reading has made me a lifelong learner.

I still automatically read everything I see, although it's becoming harder for my aging eyes to distinguish smaller print or lighter print. I specifically don't read Doonesbury comics because I have to squint to figure out what the characters are saying. Sometimes, in dim situations, I try to "pass" because I can't really read the program or the instructions.

And what's the benefit of all this so-called knowing? Is it so that, for some obscure reason, others will like me? Or so that I will like myself?

What if, in fact, I don't know? What if all my opinions turn out to be useless? What if my well-trained ideas turn out to be mere statistical guesses?

The ego wants to know, wants to know things for sure. As if there were such a thing as certainty. Not-knowing gives rise to a low level of anxiety. *Oh no! I don't actually know what's going to happen* — tonight, tomorrow, next week.

Although I believe in the truth of knowing, perhaps not-knowing is actually more true. I don't know where and how this piece of writing will end, although I'd like to tie it up in a neat bow. I don't really know what I'm saying here.

The eyes grow old. I try to compensate with bifocals, with reading glasses.

One doesn't need glasses to read the world, to enjoy today's day, to listen to the cardinal singing or the forsythia blooming. Read life. That's all there is, really.

TRAVELS

OUR PET NENE

38-*Across: Hawaiian goose.*

I learned the answer to this crossword puzzle clue a few decades ago: "nene."

In fact, the nene is the state bird of Hawai'i. One nature writer speculates that some Canada geese got blown off their migratory course some thousands of years ago. Once the geese landed in the Hawaiian Islands, there was nowhere to migrate to, and really no reason to go much of anywhere. Cold weather can be found on top of the 12,000-foot volcanoes on the Big Island of Hawai'i or on the 10,000-foot Haleakala volcano on Maui.

When Bill and I went to Maui, we backpacked 2,000 feet down into the Haleakala Crater and stayed at one of the three wilderness cabins there. The first thing we had to do was shoo a tenter out of the cabin's front yard and over to the campground, about 200 yards away.

NO CAMPING NEAR THE CABIN, a sign said, but both afternoons we arrived to find a tent pitched right beside the sign. "It's the only flat spot around," both men said. I nodded sympathetically. I'm a tent camper too, and some campgrounds that you actually pay good money for only offer dirt on an incline. Flat grass looks so much more inviting.

And one of the reasons this short grass looked so inviting was that a nene lived there and nibbled the lawn into good condition.

"Look, Bill," I said. "We have a pet nene." Like all native Hawaiian species, the nene is not afraid of people, since there are no native predators in Hawai'i. As I was sitting at the picnic table outside Holua cabin, the nene wandered closer and curiously closer. I saw his sleek black head and black bill with beady black eyes. Tan cheek feathers swirled down his neck into a body and behind that looked, well, like a Canadian goose, except tanner. The nene is smaller, though, not needing reserves of fat for the brief periods of refrigerator weather at 8,000 feet; at night, the temperatures at Haleakala can drop into the 30s. Two days after we hiked out, the Haleakala National Park was closed by several inches of snow.

Our nene nibbled on grass, and seemed to find other things of interest in the dirt. He was there in the yard all afternoon. Waiting for a handout? Signs plastered inside the cabin and out, as well as in all the national park brochures, practically shouted: DO NOT FEED THE NENE.

Just before bedtime (in a bunk bed that I had slept in with my Hawaiian boyfriend 38 years earlier), I went out to pee in the grass. There was Nene, walking toward me, making low humming noises, catching me in midstream as I squatted there. I hummed back.

I got up to pee again at eleven, just after the moon had risen, and that's when I recognized typical goose behavior. Nene was running at me, mouth open and tongue out, and I was squatting again. I stuck out one foot to ward it off, and it deftly veered away.

At 3:00 A.M., I squatted near its silent shape; Nene was undisturbed until it heard me watering the grass.

The next day, as we returned from our seven-hour hike around the red and black and yellow cinder cones on the bottom of the crater, we saw the cabin from a distance. But where was our Nene? We walked across a field of lava boulders, and Nene met us on the path with a couple of his friends, who were poking about the greenery between the rocks.

As we hiked away from Holua cabin on our last day, I finally realized that this goose was *not* our pet nene. Nene owned the place, and we were the intruders.

SUPAI

Our second day in the village of Supai, located naturally enough in the Supai formation, halfway down into the Grand Canyon, we had hiked the one and a half miles to Havasu Falls—the actual destination for this trip. Caribbean-blue water pouring over the red rock juxtaposed desert and water, heat and coolness, aridity and, yes, close to Havasu Creek, a palpable humidity.

We had walked through the 200-site campground that was fed by a single potable water source—Fern Spring. We saw maybe ten tents, all near the spring, but picnic tables meandered close to the creek for another quarter mile.

The travertine terraces that pond the water at the base of the falls had been blown out by a flash flood two years ago and had been replaced by sandbags. Already a quarter inch of the calcium carbonate travertine had formed in some spots—Nature on her way to redecorating this sandstone-and-aqua room, graced by green cottonwoods and shrub willows. Bits of calcium carbonate flowed into our water shoes as we walked through the water from lagoon to pondlet, water pouring over a one-foot waterfall that we could jacuzzi our well-hiked bodies in.

After an hour or two, we shouldered our day-packs over our wet clothes and walked on to the next falls, one half mile to Mooney Falls—at 210 feet, taller than Niagara. I had heard about the ladders on the cliff and didn't know if I would be able to clamber down. Bill, of course, has no fear of heights. He bungee-jumped in New Zealand for his seventieth birthday. We had hiked the eight miles into Supai for his seventy-fifth.

The trail began descending over ancient travertine terraces formed, perhaps, at the end of the last ice age when there was enough water to make Mooney Falls as wide as Niagara. Now all that remained was travertine drapery, as if a 300-yard-wide waterfall had turned to stone in midair. Ten thousand years of red dust from the Hermit Shale layered above the Supai formation had painted the limestone travertine the same color as the Supai sandstone.

I came to a hand-painted sign: DESCEND AT OWN RISK.

"Just an old mine," I called to Bill, but then I looked again and saw light just 15 feet down. I clambered down the hand-hewn steps of various heights and various widths, feeling my way with my hiking poles.

The light found me standing on a two-foot by two-foot stone balcony, about 15 stories high, just beside an overhang of travertine curtains, as if I had just made my entry on stage. Thick chains were anchored into the rock on both sides of the next set of unequal and unpredictable handholds and footholds. Hiking poles are useless and even dangerous in these sorts of rock-climbing situations. I turned to face the rock, looped my poles around my left wrist, held onto the chains for dear life, and began to descend backwards.

In some moments the chains swayed a bit; in others they held firm. Then I came to a homemade wooden ladder of four steps. Oh, the relief of predictability! I threw my poles out and down to the ground, 50 feet below, hoping they wouldn't stick in some unreachable place. Then more chains, more footholds, down step by step until I came to an aluminum ladder standing on flat ground. Oh, I could do that, all right. Down the ladder, past one rung that had been replaced by a thick stick wired in place.

Wriggling out of our day-packs, we splashed into the cool turquoise-blue water again.

―

That early evening in Supai, back at the lodge, we lay prostrate on our bed, air conditioner on high.

"You know," I said, "if you set a match to this place, it would be a torch in 30 seconds." I had just noticed the sizable cracks in the bone-dry wooden threshold under our door. The siding looked parched. The wooden window frames would turn to splinters if I applied even a little pressure to open the windows.

Then I heard a big bang. *Fireworks?* I wondered, without following that thought to its logical conclusion. Bang! Bang!

"Ready for dinner, Bill?" We walked out our door and saw a group of fellow tourists gathered on the western deck of the lodge.

Bang!

We walked that way to see a fire burning behind a heavy chain-link fence about 50 yards away.

"It's the trash," someone said.

Bang!

"So those are aerosol cans exploding?" I asked.

Bang! Bang!

Someone answered, "Probably those camping propane canisters."

Bang!

Probably lots of plastic bags and plastic water bottles, I thought.

Bill and I walked on toward the cafe. Just then a Havasupai man roared up on an ATV that had a little four-foot by four-foot bed behind it. He took a wrench and opened a faded fire hydrant and attached a fire hose. Other Caucasians appeared—the minister of the Bible Chapel, a nurse, a teacher. The Havasupai man threw six fire hoses on the ground and roared off. Four of us sprang to the hoses and began to roll them out, unkink them, and flatten them. I kept looking over my shoulder at the nearby Supai Fire Department shed. The door remained closed.

"I don't think there's anything in it," said the nurse.

Bang! Bang!

Where were the Havasupai?

"This is the third time the trash has caught on fire this summer," someone else said.

The hoses attached and screwed together still came about 75 feet short of reaching the fire.

A young Havasupai walking from the trail maintenance department behind the lodge said, "Last time we angled the hose through the brush. That way it'll come closer." He stood there, hands at his side, waiting for someone in authority to make a decision. Two other women and I began hauling the hose, as if we'd made a silent group decision, and the young Havasupai man ran the hose through the brush, leaving one dysfunctional hose lying in the dust.

"Let's go eat," said Bill. "I don't see why we should be doing this."

I brushed my dusty hands together as I watched the water swell into the hose and toward the fire. A little

Bobcat bulldozer from the maintenance shed ran toward the chain-link fence containing the fire and knocked the gate open. The Bobcat drove in, but immediately backed out. Driven back by the heat? By the exploding shrapnel of propane canisters?

"Come on, Cheryl," said Bill. "I'm hungry."

I brushed my still-dusty hands against my shorts. An arc of water sprayed toward the fire. It looked like this would take a while. A low-lying cloud of white smoke began to drift toward the village.

"Let's go, Cheryl," said Bill. "I don't want to breathe that smoke. Just think what it has in it."

I finally turned my back on the fire and walked away with Bill, through the village of the People of the Blue-Green Waters.

BRITISH SOUP

After a month at a meditation retreat in England with oatmeal for breakfast and soup for dinner, 28 days in a row, here's my verdict on British soups: They come in the same colors as British living room décor—pea-soup green, parsnip-soup beige, and pumpkin-soup gold. I never did work up my nerve to try the celeriac soup.

The soups were uniformly thick, as if the cooks in the kitchen had taken the leftover kale from lunch, run it through a food processor, and simply heated it up for dinner.

The soup bowls were large—the size of small mixing bowls that took two large ladles to fill. The whole-wheat bread was sliced thick and slathered with butter and jam or Marmite.

My American friend in London, Nancy, had warned me, "The Brits love their root vegetables. And they love leeks."

She was right. I saw leeks almost every day, either served as a vegetable side dish or flavoring the main course. Never had I eaten parsnips so often—as the veg course at lunch, then ground into thick soup for dinner. Carrots, of course, but never a dainty finger-sized one. Potatoes in all forms. And the occasional rutabaga.

Soup was just what was needed when the sun set at four o'clock, and wind blew so fiercely over the moors that drafts poured in all the single-pane windows. After a simple supper of soup, I sat and sipped a proper cup of tea in the lounge, which was decorated in pea green, parsnip beige, and pumpkin gold.

FAR NORTH

Bill and I love to vacation in the Far North during the weeks around summer solstice. We started the tradition by camping on the Icefields Parkway that connects Banff to Jasper on the eastern edge of British Columbia. After dinner around the camp stove on the picnic table, we'd hike for an hour or two. By the time we cozied into our sleeping bags at eleven o'clock, we still didn't need a headlamp to read inside the tent. But it was a bit disconcerting to answer the bladder's call at 3:00 A.M. and find I was peeing in a tundra of birches in broad daylight.

We traveled to Iceland and hiked along a river, passing 22 waterfalls in the four miles it took to reach the edge of the snow. In Reykjavik, we watched the sun finally set at midnight from the top of La Perla—four round water towers that supply the city with hot water for heating homes. Two hours later, we were asleep at sunrise. The following year, we flew to the north side of Iceland, above the Arctic Circle, where they have an all-night golf tournament on summer solstice.

We've flown to Alaska four times and gone as far north as Fairbanks, but in the summer the weather is mostly cloudy, so we didn't take a flight to the Arctic Circle. We've seen a whale mama teaching her baby how to dive and a seal mama on a little iceberg reaching out to comfort her anxious baby with her flipper. *There, there, now.* While rafting the Tanana River in central Alaska, Bill jumped into the 33-degree water in a dry suit and floated beside the raft for ten minutes. In Anchorage, I couldn't take my eyes off the huge hanging baskets of cobalt-blue lobelia, as well as the oversized columbines, cabbages, and pumpkins.

One summer we traveled with Stephen Stearns, our local clown, and 35 Russian orphans on a boat from Moscow, up the Volga, past Lake Ladoga, north through 69 locks to the White Sea and the Solovetsky islands, where the biggest island, Solovki, had been a part of the gulag archipelago. Grim. But walking around the city of Petrozavodsk ("Peter's Factory") in our clown costumes was great fun.

The next year, while I still remembered the Russian alphabet, we went to Finland and Estonia, and then ended in St. Petersburg for the White Nights. At ten P.M. people suddenly outnumbered the cars on the broad boulevard of Nevsky Prospekt. Then the traffic disappeared completely, replaced by a throng of people walking north to the square outside the Hermitage, where the music and the party continued through the dusk that turned to dawn a few hours later.

Beautiful Stockholm, scattered over many islands, delighted us with a variety of attractions. We then spent a week on Gotland with its surprising riviera, in the middle of the shallow (and therefore relatively warm) Baltic Sea. People picked bouquets of wildflowers from the roadsides for *Midsommar* festivals, and birch saplings decorated the corners of houses, barns, and even mini-marts to give good health to those within. Maypoles, dancing, and drinking closed all the shops and businesses (even the hotel where we were staying) in this annual polar opposite of Christmas.

But Norway wins my prize for farthest north. We took the ferry named Hurtigruten (think: *hurtling route*) north from the spectacular Geiranger fjord. Day after day, night after light night, the boat stopped at villages to unload supplies and take on local people and their cars. On summer solstice we crossed the Arctic Circle and still continued north. We disembarked 250 kilometers later, at Trömsö, and went to a concert at eleven P.M. in a modern church. Streaks of stained-glass light traveled across the walls as the music calmed us, and we emerged at midnight to full sun high in the sky. Surprisingly, Trömsö feels the effect of the Gulf Stream, so they say it isn't that cold in the winter.

North and north again—where summer days last as long as months.

ON VACATION—AGAIN

Bill and I are on vacation—again. Right now we're in Belize. But I always feel a bit uneasy when people ask, "Oh! Are you going on vacation?"

Bill and I are both retired. We lead fulfilling lives. What exactly do we need a vacation *from*?

Bill doesn't need a vacation from his piano. In fact, he spends his time in the rental car playing the piano on his knees. He calls it "practicing finger dexterity and finger independence." He laments having lost the memory of the sonata he had up to tempo just before we left for our vacation. He's been playing it on his knees and in his mind every day, but after a week he's lost the difficult passages. Bill doesn't need or even want a vacation from his piano.

He is always looking for a piano to practice on, but tropical places, like Belize, are not really good places for pianos—it's too humid. At home, Bill humidifies his piano studio in the winter, and he de-humidifies it in the summer, always aiming for a perfect 50 percent reading on the humidistat on the piano.

Plus, pianos are now out of fashion. I cannot tell you how many hotels and bars we have walked into in Bill's search for a piano. "Oh, we just got rid of the piano last week," they often say. "It used to sit right there." They point to an empty, piano-sized space in the lobby or conference room.

I don't want a vacation from my meditation practice; it's hard to keep it going while traveling. I often sit up in bed, on my bed pillow, at 6:00 A.M., with my knee jutting into Bill's neck while he snoozes. I sit for 20, or sometimes 30, minutes. But often there are get-up-and-go mornings, especially when we're in transit, when there's repacking to do, and meditation just drops out of my routine.

Bill doesn't need a vacation from his Rotary meetings, which he enjoys for their old-boy camaraderie. Visiting other Rotary clubs is just not the same—especially when it's in a foreign language.

I don't need a vacation from my writing group. If anything, I need more occasions to write, not fewer.

Bill and I don't need a vacation from our yoga class. Bill is good at doing daily exercises for his back, so he gets in 20 minutes of stretching each day. I'm too involved with my vacation activities—reading a novel or doing a sudoku or knitting while I'm waiting for Bill—so yoga and walking drop out of sight.

Bill doesn't need a vacation from hiking and biking. He's at the use-it-or-lose-it age, when physical exercise is essential to life. A friend's 90-year-old mother walks five miles a day. All her friends who don't walk are dead.

I don't need a vacation from my gardens. In fact, I refuse to go on vacation in April and May because of all the work the gardens need then.

Why should we vacate our beautiful house in the vacation destination of Vermont? The scenery is lovely here, and there are plenty of vacation-y activities nearby. We can zip-line down a ski hill in the summer or ski down it in the winter. We can kayak or swim in ponds or rivers. We can climb mountains or ride bikes on rail trails. The four seasons are beautiful here.

What Bill and I *do* need a vacation for is to spend time with each other. At home we are often two ships passing in the night. I get up hours before he does, and he comes to bed an hour after I've gone to sleep. "Feel you later," he often says as he heads out to another evening meeting on social justice, saving a green space, the Conservation Commission, the Planning Commission, or the Dummerston Trails Committee.

In the morning I return from my morning meditation group and a walk through the woods to find Bill enjoying his hour-long breakfast and listening to classical music. I'm ready to go to work on my computer, focusing on a writing project or doing my own bookkeeping. At 10:00 A.M. he plays the piano for an hour and then makes phone calls before he leaves to deliver Meals on Wheels.

I surface for lunch by myself, then attend to afternoon appointments — my hospice client on Tuesday, breathwork on Wednesday, a massage on Thursday. I don't need a vacation from any of these.

If we're lucky, Bill and I will fall into bed together for our afternoon nap, and we wake together after 20 minutes. Then we go in separate directions until dinner time.

On vacation we're together 24/7. That's what we need a vacation for: each other.

BILL

MYRTLE

I was away from home for three hours yesterday. That's all — just three hours — and that's all it took for Bill to weed the myrtle out from under the PJM rhododendron.

This is a man who never weeds. We have fallen into our natural domains — I do the gardens, he does the trees. The system works well to create an environment of lovely gardens. I work from eye level down; he works from eye level up. He cuts down beech saplings to reveal the white birch just behind them. He trims hemlocks into Christmas trees or into hedges, making beautiful backgrounds for the flowers in front.

In fact, I fell in love with Bill because of his pruning. I'd never seen a multi-branched avocado tree that looked like a shrub, but there it stood in his office, branches gracefully drooping in all directions. I thought I wanted a man who could cook, but pruning turned out to be more important.

So I wasn't surprised that he wanted to prune the PJM rhododendron at the corner of the garage. I didn't agree with it, but sometimes I just have to leave him to his own devices. "Bill, I can't bear to look. Just prune it when I'm not looking," I tell him. I hold that avocado tree in my memory as the talisman that whatever he takes his clippers to will turn out all right.

We met in town, and he proudly told me his accomplishments of the past few hours.

"Ripping out the myrtle!" I said, looking at him with steely eyes. "How could you? That was uncalled for." And what was he doing down at ground level anyway?

"Bill!" I continued. "That was a special myrtle with *purple* flowers, not blue flowers. The grape color coordinates beautifully with the PJM's pinky-purple blossoms, and they bloom at the same time. I was trying to get the PJM to have a purple skirt. Besides, the myrtle is self-contained there. It can't go anywhere because it's surrounded by driveway. What *were* you thinking?"

"Well, it was weedy there, so I just ripped everything out," he said.

"Including the lobelia and the meadow rue?" I asked.

"Hmmm. I guess so."

"What were you *thinking*?" I asked.

"Well, this is my area," he said.

"It is? That's why I've been taking care of it for the past 20 years?"

"It's next to the garage where I park my car," he said.

I heaved a sigh and rolled my eyes. "Bill. Usually we consult with each other. What possessed you to just rip out the myrtle?"

"It was weedy," he said.

I could tell he was digging in his heels. I couldn't make him wrong. He wanted to be right. And I wanted to be right.

"I am so mad at you," I said.

He folded his arms across his chest.

An hour later, we were home, and Bill showed me his handiwork. He had pulled the so-called weeds out, but myrtle isn't that easy to get rid of. It was stealthily lying in ambush beneath the PJM.

"You've been building up the soil here," Bill said accusingly.

"Well, I mulch the PJM with pine needles to acidify the soil and counteract the lime that's leaching out of the cement footing," I said.

"But the water runs into the garage," Bill said. "I've got to direct the water away from the garage."

"Bill," I said. "The PJM acts like a rain garden, slowing down the flow of water."

We had done our best to out-logic each other, but the rationales were a draw.

Eventually, I managed to calm myself down. This kind of thing will happen more and more as I grow older and less able to care for the gardens. Other people will make decisions that I think are ignorant. They'll have their reasons, and they'll think that they are right.

And this is just the way life unfolds, year to year, garden to garden, lifetime to lifetime.

SIDDIE'S EIGHTIETH BIRTHDAY

B ILL PLAYED A concert for his favorite girlfriend from his twenties, Siddie. He called her husband a month before Siddie's eightieth birthday and said he wanted to come down to Brookline, Massachusetts, and celebrate by playing for Siddie on her beautiful Steinway piano. A day later his offer had turned into a recital for 40 of their closest friends. Bill had recently performed the same concert at the home of a friend in Brattleboro, so he already had the music in his fingers.

He planned to end Siddie's concert with a surprise. In fact, he had planned all the details, but in typical Bill fashion—or should I say lack of fashion?—surprising things happened.

He wanted to leave home at eleven thirty on Sunday morning, so we negotiated a compromise. I would give a Dharma talk in Brattleboro, and he'd pick me up there at noon. I ended the talk five minutes early and dashed out the door, leaving six people to close up the room. As they drove away, one by one, I was sitting in my car waiting for Bill, who eventually arrived out-of-breath at twelve thirty.

He's usually on time, or even early, for musical events, and late for everything else. It's a good thing that I've been practicing patience for the past year.

We arrived in Brookline at three, and Bill sat down at

the piano to rehearse. When the first guest came, he ran upstairs to change his suit. As the last guests were arriving at four, Bill came downstairs in his bow tie and whispered to me, "Look at this suit!"

Hmmm. It didn't look like the silk suit he had had made in Thailand three years ago. Nope. He'd grabbed the suit my sister had picked out for him for my dad's funeral in 1997—back when oversized and double-breasted were in. He stretched his arms and the cuffs still hit him below the wrists. "The sleeves will drag on the keys," he said.

"Take your jacket off when you sit down to play," I told him.

"And look!" he said, pointing to his feet. "I thought I had my black shoes."

I looked down to brown Birkenstocks and shook my head. "No one will be looking at your feet," I consoled him.

"Yes, but look at the socks!" he said. He was wearing one black sock and one navy blue sock.

Bill entered the living room to applause, played two Saint-Saëns bagatelles, a Schumann sonata, and a lovely rhapsody by Brahms. He stood up to take his bow. "I met Siddie in 1959," he said. "And I had the pleasure of escorting her to the Boston Viennese Waltz evenings. So for my encore I'd like to wear the tuxedo I wore those evenings." He magically pulled Liberace tails out of a box on the floor. The jacket fit him like a glove.

"And," he said, "for that occasion, Siddie made herself an evening gown. Later, she gave it to me for my future waltzing partners to wear." He didn't mention that he was the Waltzing Champion of Boston in 1959. "So here, Siddie. I'm returning your dress to you."

Out of another box, he pulled a floor-length dress with a green velvet bodice and a sea-green crepe skirt. Size 4. Bill sat down at the piano and played a short waltz for the woman he loved in 1959.

And still loves.

FLIRTERS

Flirting. Oh! Is that what's happening when I feel certain that if I were available, that man would ask me out on a date? I've felt that way around Bill's friend Larry for the past 20 years. For the first five years, Larry had a different girlfriend every year. He remained friends with the ex-girlfriends even with a new one on his arm. Wow. How did he do that?

Then he met Sandy, who is 20 years younger, and she has stayed in the picture even when I've seen Larry with other women. Three years ago he was the last to arrive at my birthday party, and he came with a new woman, Judy, on his arm. She looked to be about his age, and they looked like they "fit" together.

Larry introduced her to me and Bill. As she took Bill's hand, she leaned into him and whispered, "Billy."

"Judy!" Bill nearly shouted. "You're the girl who taught me how to kiss."

All of a sudden, I was a wallflower at a convention of flirters. Pretty sweet when a 71-year-old woman has two men fawning over her. Judy knew how to take center stage, and carry the conversation as she talked about the 50 years since she and Bill had seen each other. The conversation bounced along, skimming over the people they knew in common.

"Oh, yes," Judy said. "I called Dede when my daughter died, but she was on retreat, and they wouldn't let me through."

"You and Dede used to be thick as thieves," Bill said. "You've stayed in touch with her?"

"Oh yes," Judy said. "You know she married Peter Bull."

"I went to school with him," Bill said. "I never did think that was a good match. She was so sweet, and he was so dull. Dede invited me to their wedding, but I just couldn't bear to go. I never saw her after that."

"Well, they divorced," Judy said. "And she changed her name. Now she's Pema Chödrön."

"Pema Chödrön!*" I shouted from the sidelines.

"Who's that?" asked Bill.

Judy took the conversational ball and kept it rolling. The flirters knew how to keep each other in a feel-good frame of mind.

---

* Pema Chödrön became a Buddhist nun in 1974 after two divorces. She is the author of

- *The Wisdom of No Escape*
- *Start Where You Are: A Guide to Compassionate Living*
- *When Things Fall Apart: Heart Advice for Difficult Times*
- *The Places That Scare You: A Guide to Fearlessness in Difficult Times*
- *Comfortable with Uncertainty*
- *No Time to Lose*
- *Practicing Peace in Times of War.*

TRAPPING

Bill is the official trapper in our house. "What would you do without me?" he asks.

What he means is that every morning, after meditation, I take the Buddhist vow of non-harming—the vow not to destroy life. Then I open my eyes and watch Bill carry a dead mouse *en*-trap out to the woods at the edge of the lawn. He flings the body into the trees. Later in the morning I look out the window to see a feral cat napping by the fishpond.

"Look Bill," I whisper loudly. But at the sound of voices and movement—even muffled by four walls—the white-and-gray cat's eyes open, and she slinks out of sight behind the iris.

I turn on the water in the sink and glare at the ant traps on the window sill, very near the tomatoes that are sitting there. "Bill," I say. "These ant traps..."

"They're doing a good job, aren't they?" he says. "I just put some more of them under the cabinets."

I lean over to see three of them located strategically in the corners, and under the refrigerator.

By this time Bill is finishing his breakfast, flyswatter in hand. "Cheryl! You have to close the doors," he chides me. I haven't been leaving them open.

"I've dispatched 20 flies this morning," he declares. "You know what I think?"

"No, Bill," I say. "I never know what you're thinking."

"I think it's that fish emulsion you use to fertilize your houseplants."

I pause. I never would have come up with that theory, not in a hundred years of flies, but now that he mentions it, I can almost imagine it. Dead fish in Maine, flies, machines grinding piles of dead sea life into a stinky brown glop. Would fly eggs survive in that white plastic gallon jug of fish emulsion? And don't the eggs have to turn into maggots first?

But before I can complete that train of thought, Bill has dashed out the door to chase a red squirrel off the deck. I sigh my way upstairs, and then I hear him shouting in excited syllables. "Hoo!" "Ah!" "No!" "Get out of here!" "Ha!"

Is he having a seizure? Or a heart attack? By the time I gallop downstairs, he is roaring with laughter. "A red squirrel ran into the house, all around the kitchen, through the dining room, all over the plants in your greenhouse, and out the greenhouse door. All in less than 30 seconds." He smiles, and then he says, "I've got to put out a trap for that red squirrel."

Bill catches red squirrels—and chipmunks—in a Hav-a-Heart trap and deports them to swamps and forests at least two miles away from our house. He has tried using Hav-a-Heart traps for mice, but can't bear the suffering of the mice, which often die of fright before he finds them in the trap. He feels it's more humane to snap-trap them.

Three years ago, while pawing through our tall camping equipment box, full of sleeping bags and sleeping mats, down at the very bottom I felt a . . . walnut? Odd. I pulled out a perfect mouse skeleton, complete with tiny toe bones and a long tail bone. I keep this miniature skeleton on the window sill near the front door to remind me that, like the mice, I too am of the nature to die—suddenly or slowly, painlessly or painfully.

Suffering is in the mind of the beholder.

BEST OF THE BLOG:

The Daily Edition of
The Meditative Gardener

www.themeditativegardener.blogspot.com

Follow *The Meditative Gardener* on Facebook.

GARDENING IN THE SNOW

My 84-year-old friend, Trudy Crites, tells me winter is the time to scatter poppy seeds, when my flower beds are covered with a foot of snow.

You know how you feel when you hear truth?

Something inside relaxes. *Oh! Yes.* The body relaxes; then the mind gets busy and tells you a story. The mind is so entertaining and the story so believable (even if it's not true), that it's easy to miss that initial body response of calmness.

Regarding poppies, I have tried scattering seeds in the cold mud of April—a month before the last frost date here in the North Country. I've never quite been satisfied with the results. In late autumn, I've seen teensy-weensy two-leaved poppies volunteering, so I know they like to get an early start. Really early.

I'm strapping on my snowshoes right now to go out to the garden and plant poppy seeds.

THE SNOWPLOW DOES SOME GARDENING FOR ME

Living in the North Country means having your driveway snowplowed after every snowfall. Herein comes the dilemma: the snowplow or the garden?

To defend my kitchen garden at the end of the driveway from the winter's moraine of driveway gravel, I installed two sections of fence separated by an arbor—a lovely transition from the parking area to a green and flowering "room" during spring, summer, and fall.

The male in my household comes down firmly on the side of the snowplow and faithfully removes the fence sections every November. In April, after snowmelt, I may have to remind him to replace the walls of my herb garden "room".

Every spring I find that the snowplow has done some gardening for me. Three years ago, I found a hosta growing in the woods. How did it get there? It took me a while to piece together the story of the snowplow nicking it out of the side of the driveway and bulldozing it into the huge snow fort at the end of his run. Incredibly the hosta survived. As did a lady fern the following year.

This year I found mitella (miterwort) and lamium refugees from my white garden at the front door camped about 20 feet away in a grove of maidenhair fern.

Of course, the question is not *either* the snowplow *or* the garden. The answer is: the snowplow *and* the garden.

SLEEPING ON A CLOUD

Last night
I slept
on a cloud,
shimmering stars
above me,
misty firmament below.

The cherry-pink dawn
woke me to spring
scintillating ice crystals
of the chill and bird-swept land.

LET'S PLANT

Perennial Swappers has its first meeting of the season in mid-April. The gardening season begins! Let's plant!

The first evening we don't swap perennials, as we do at every bi-weekly meeting from May through September. Instead we watch Bruce Bellville of Meetinghouse Gardens, a wholesaler, divide plants. Every year he teaches us how to divide big clumps while he tells us garden lore. Then he sells the divisions for $1 or $2 or $3. Big clumps of hellebores — 8 varieties — for $3 each.

This meeting is a good place to watch desire arising. "Ooh. I want *that*." In the name of fairness, everyone who gets in line for the ruffled iris or the variegated sedum can buy only one. If there are leftovers, we can get in line again and buy one more, and so on until no more divisions remain.

Watching people's kindness toward each other is inspiring. "Here, you get in line ahead of me. I already have one of these."

Anytime we show our concern for others, anytime we give "me-first" a rest, we are watering the seeds of kindness.

THE ILLUSION OF CONTROL

In May, while the growing season is still in its childhood, our hearts open wide toward our gardens. Now we train them toward what we imagine will be perfect beauty and yield.

The willfulness of weeds and even the proliferation of the young plants themselves are only beginning. We think we can keep up with them.

But alas! The youthful vigor of our gardens exceeds our own energy. Too soon we turn our attention to the workaday world and leave our latchkey gardens to their own devices. By July, we are clucking our tongues over their unruly behavior. "But what can we do?" we say to our friends.

But in May, we are in love, we believe in our hopes and dreams for the future, and that is sufficient.

MY HONEY LOVES BEES

My honey has fallen in love with bees this spring. He walks out the front door toward his car, and comes to a halt beside the rhododendron, where a dozen bumblebees are rolling around in the pinky-purple blossoms.

In the past, he has run away from bees as fast as possible, waving his arms about his head. He has dared me to mow near the nests of ground bees—and I have done so unscathed. I walk near bees calmly. I walk in beauty. And so far they haven't bothered me.

My heart is warmed by seeing my honey's goodwill toward bees. Maybe it's the bee pollen he's been eating on his cereal every morning for the past month in an effort to ward off spring allergies. This year, he enjoys watching the bees roll around in flower pollen. This year he is literally one with the bees and their pollen.

MORE RAIN

Rain
and more rain.
Water pouring from the sky
day after day
leaking all over my plans
to garden
and drenching bean plants
in the garden.

Drowning blackflies and mosquitoes by day;
grounding fireflies at night.

Summer beckons from the calendar,
but refrigerator weather
suspends us in this so-long spring.

We're all wet
if we think for a moment
the weather should be different
than it is.

LIGHTNING BUGS

I ALWAYS ASSUMED fireflies were called "lightning bugs" because they flash on and off like sparks of lightning. But the name "lightning bugs" took on a new meaning one night in June as several cells of thunderstorms passed over in quick succession. I say "thunderstorms" because drenching rain was accompanied by heat lightning, but I actually heard very little thunder.

In between downpours, during an interval of misty sprinkling, lightning lit up the entire sky for half a second. After every switch-on/switch-off of lightning, the lady lightning bugs lounging in the grass blinked on in a chorus of orgasms.

Then darkness fell all around, suddenly lit by a bowl of lightning overhead. Three seconds later, the lady lightning bugs switched on as if the grass were covered with strings of fairy lights.

Lightning bugs responding to lightning.
Earth echoing heaven's song of light.

THE PHOE-BE SONG

A PHOEBE WAGS its tail as it sits on the back of a lawn chair. This perch gives it a bird's-eye view of the insects flying around two feet above the yard. It zooms out, seems to snap at thin air, returns to the lawn chair, and swallows. Mosquitoes? Blackflies?

The phoebe never comes to the bird feeders. It builds its nest in an eave of the house (hopefully not near the bedroom window), and sings its raucous "phoe-be" song as if it has laryngitis.

Two chickadees have taken up residence in a bluebird house near the vegetable garden. They flit back and forth to the entrance, apparently feeding babies. Sometimes one of them sits on the wire fence and sings its melodic "phoeeeeee-beeeeeeee" song, dropping half a step between "phoeeee" and "beeeee."

Two unrelated birds singing a very similar song—one unpleasant, one very pleasant.

There's no need to wish the unpleasant away nor to desire more of the pleasant. Birds simply sing their songs, and mindfulness simply listens.

A RARE WHITE VIOLET

My friend Barbara and I went out in July to look for a particular endangered violet. We are Plant Conservation Volunteers with the New England Wild Flower Society. I had been to this Lily Pond seven years ago with another volunteer/friend, and we found the Bog White Violet (*Viola lanceolata*) growing just where it was supposed to be—three feet above the water line. This year—nothing.

Barbara and I traipsed back and forth along the edge of the pond and found lots of evidence of beavers—an old dam; dozens of chewed sticks with the bark stripped off of them; several beaver slides leading into the pond; birches as big as eight inches in diameter felled by beavers and then "sawed" into various log lengths. Fascinating to see the tooth chiselings on the wood. This walking around in circles often happens in the hunt for rare plants; it's like looking for a needle in a haystack. We searched and wondered how to explain the disappearance of 300 plants. Was the water level higher?

We were just about to resign from our task. Near the beaver dam, I was standing on one foot and then the other, waiting for Barbara-the-naturalist to identify various sedges. I looked down. "Well, here at least is a white violet," I said.

Barbara came to look; I looked more closely at the long pointy leaves. *Viola lanceolata*! About 35 plants, growing three feet above a little mud flat behind the old (and leaky) beaver dam.

Our actions and the results of our actions reseed themselves in this manner. Even after we are gone, like the rare violet no longer growing near the water's edge, the results of our actions will have reseeded themselves elsewhere and taken root.

Let us do our best to act as beautifully as the little white violet.

DIFFERENT GARDENING STYLES

When I go outdoors in the mornings, I stroll around my flowerbeds, clippers in one hand, bucket in the other. I'm deadheading and propping up flowers, and generally tidying up some flowerbed or other.

At 7:45, I arrive for meditation at my neighbor Connie's, and there she is in her nightgown hauling foot-tall (or more!) weeds out of her vegetable gardens, her hands caked with dirt, and her white nightie pretty well smudged.

For me, flowers are the priority; for her, vegetables.

The mind loves to compare. So far as I can see, that's *all* the mind actually does. And in this comparison, the mind wants to divide the world into good and bad, black and white, better and worse. Yet here are Connie and I, two old friends with very different gardening styles, both reaping joy.

A TASTE OF HEAVEN

I TAKE ALL my houseplants outdoors for their summer vacation—all, except one: the hoya or wax plant. It continues to hang under a skylight in the solarium, its vines nearly touching their toes to the floor.

The upside-down umbrella of pale pink waxy star-shaped flowers neatly interlock with one another. Each pale pink star is centered with a white star which has a perfect tiny red flower at its center and in the center of the red, a tiny white tongue secretes one clear drop of sweet syrup. Touch your tongue to it for a taste of ambrosia, mildly flavored by the hoya's perfume.

That's the real reason I keep it indoors in the summer. When I walk into the house at night, it smells like I've walked into heaven.

BIRD BRANCH

A FEW FEET away from the bird feeder on our deck, I have attached a dead branch to an upright post that supports the railing. The dead branch may not be very attractive to humans, but birds love it. They perch on any of its various twigs before, and sometimes after, grabbing a sunflower seed from the feeder.

Eating dinner on the deck, my sweetie and I sometimes proceed in freeze frame. Fork halfway to mouth stops in midair in order not to scare away the rose-breasted grosbeak. The situation calls for mindfulness. Sometimes I move, millimeter by millimeter—a form of mindful movement.

But I don't tell the chickadees that I'm having chicken for dinner.

APPRECIATIVE JOY

I'M CRAWLING AROUND the vegetable garden on my hands and knees so I can get a better look at a little brown bird that is sitting on top of a fence post and singing his heart out to the four directions. Miraculously he sits and sings till I'm crouching among the bush beans and close enough to gaze at him.

He stops singing and preens himself unselfconsciously, spreading his wing feathers to clean between them like I do with my toes. Then he just sits and watches. I hear the hum of bees and see one rolling around in a nearby poppy. Gnat-size blackflies hover near my face. I hear the zoom of a hummingbird nearby.

I recite the new Appreciative Joy phrases I learned at a recent meditation retreat. "How wonderful you are in your being. . . . I delight that you are here."

This nondescript little brown bird *is* wonderful. My heart swells, drinking in the late summer afternoon. Then the plain brown bird puffs out his breast and sings to the west. He hops around and sings to the east.

Each of us in our own way, we are both suffusing our world with joy.

DIRT IN THE TRUNK

SEPTEMBER IS THE season to make the last trip to the nursery or garden center to buy those perennials or shrubs that can hardly wait to shrug off their containers, like a coat grown too small.

Great deals are there for the spending, under the disguise of "Save 50%!" We could save 100 percent by not buying anything, but desire trumps logic any day.

So we load plants into the trunk of our car, maybe overflowing onto the floor of the back seat. Some women carry the protection of an old shower curtain or an old rug, but I always was an *au naturel* girl. After I arrive home and unload, crumbs of dirt and a dead leaf or two remind me day after day, week after week, to clean up after myself.

Desire is the culprit that weakens our integrity, that pushes us to tell a white lie, to fudge a bit, to keep the incorrect change that is given, to kill pests because we hate them, to drink one too many glasses of wine.

Our conscience knows. Our conscience has the integrity to notice our crummy behavior. But we throw those thoughts into the trunks of our mind and try not to notice.

When we finally get around to cleaning up our act, and decide to live according to our conscience, we feel so much better. Ahhh. We can breathe again.

CHILI VERMONT

TOMATILLOS. I SUPPOSE they really should be grown south of the border, at least south of the border of Vermont, where I live. But these green tomatoes inside a papery husk reseed themselves prolifically in my vegetable garden. So I let them have their way because I love chili verde. The green sauce and green salsa that you find in Mexican restaurants are made with tomatillos.

In August and September I dice them into homemade salsa. Now I'm cleaning up the vegetable garden in preparation for the first frost and harvesting hundreds of these tomatillos still in their green husks. I store them in my unheated basement, and they will last until this time next year. No canning. No freezing. All I have to do is remember that I have fresh vegetables downstairs, waiting to jump into the chili pot, roll into goulash or spike into Spanish rice. Anytime I would normally cook with tomatoes in the winter, I use tomatillos instead.

So when I go back to the garden to that profusion of tomatillo vines, and I frown, "Ai-yai-yai! What was I thinking when I didn't weed these out in June?" I just have to change the accent. "Ai-yai-yai-yai. *Canta, no llores.*" I'll sing for my supper—Chili Verde-mont tonight.

FOUR-SEASON GARDENING

I'VE BEEN PART of a community garden this summer, but before we even started, a local farmer came to talk to the six of us. "There's the spring garden, the summer garden, and the fall garden," he said.

We were particularly glad to hear about the summer garden since we had already missed the spring garden by a wide swath. It was July 1 when the first person planted the first seed. Well, actually she'd been nurturing squash plants, cucumber vines, and tomatoes in pots on her patio. She was really happy to put those babies in the ground.

And, by the way, I was really happy that she planted her extra butternut squash seedlings in my nine-by-twelve plot.

By August, she had bought herself a small freezer in which to put her abundant harvest.

In my vegetable garden at home, I clear away the summer vegetables in anticipation of the first frost. Suddenly, I see the fall garden that's been hiding underneath and behind all that green and browning camouflage. Rainbow chard, carrots, beets, broccoli, and kale. One pumpkin vine has run amok, twisting around the garden like intestines, and I have the best pumpkin crop I've ever had. Gourd vines have wound themselves over the back fence, so I have a good supply of seasonal decorations.

Spring, summer, fall. There is even a winter garden. Two years ago, my seven-year-old granddaughter wanted to go dig something out of the garden for dinner the day after Christmas. So there we were at five o'clock, flashlights in mittened-hands, digging up leeks and parsnips. A voice called to us through the dim evening, and my gardening neighbor, Connie, snowshoed up to see what we were doing. Gardening in the snow, of course.

SHROUDED IN MIST

I LIVE ON the high shoulder of a river valley, so fall mornings dawn gray to reveal rising mist. The body of the earth and, specifically, the nearby body of water are slowly losing their heat into the incoming cold air.

Summer is shifting toward winter through this intermediary season called fall. Yes, red and yellowed leaves are falling on my flowerbeds as if to season them with a dash of colored pepper. At the same time, heat is rising from earth and from water in the form of vapor.

Earth, water, air, and heat (also called fire). I watch the interplay of these four "elements" — which are actually the three forms of matter — solid, liquid, gas — plus the heat required to transubstantiate one element into another.

River water transmutes into water vapor indicating the death of summer. A slower process than the death of the physical body. One of the signs of impending death is that our body loses its heat. "People die from the feet up," my father told me. The body first withdraws heat from its extremities.

Steam rises from the teacup in my hand as I gaze out the window at the backyard, shrouded in mist.

WASTED FOOD

I HAVE THIS thing about wasting food. I don't like to do it. I'm the person who takes home a doggy bag even though I don't have a dog. I am a member of the Clean Plate Club, even though most professional women I know order salad at a restaurant and then send half of it back to the kitchen. I used to think of this as wasting food.

Then I realized that all food is "wasted." It goes into our bodies and comes out as waste. The leftovers that don't go through our bodies are also waste — going directly to the compost or garbage disposal or landfill.

Anyway you cut it, food become waste. That's just the nature of it. I don't have to clean my plate because I think I'm being kind to the food or the cook. I can be kind to my body and stop eating when I'm full.

POLITICALLY CORRECT COMPOST

I'M WORKING TOWARD my Master Composter certification and am wondering if this means that my own compost should be P.C. Politically Correct Compost would not have any bones in it. Nor would it have half-decayed woolen socks.

Since 1993, my compost has been inspired by Vera Work, a social worker and Holocaust survivor who offered a weekend workshop on Post-Traumatic Stress Disorder (PTSD) during my last semester of Counseling Psychology at Antioch University New England. Vera brought in a jar of compost that included a large rusty nail. The message to the traumatized client was clear. Everything eventually composts.

So for years I threw old ripped woolen or cotton shirts and sweaters into my compost—clothes that had no future, even in a yellow Planet Aid box. I thought they would instead aid the soil of my garden.

But then, digging into a three-year-old compost bin, I'd shovel out a more or less whole green sweater matted with fibrous roots. Maybe it wasn't wool after all? A braided rug decayed into one- or two-foot lengths. I'd pull out the braids and snake them into the neighboring bin—where I'd run into the blue woolen plaits a year or two later. Moccasins from Alaska with holes that I'd worn in the sole and the heel—the rabbit-fur lining was gone, but the leather remained. A shred of a filmy cotton blouse my mother gave me for Christmas in 1977 floats around my vegetable garden.

Now that I'm an official Master Composter, I've stopped throwing my ratty old clothes in the compost. Just last night, I tossed a holey woolen sock into the trash. Now when I pull what remains of a leather glove or the ripped sleeve of a navy blue sweater out of the compost, I put it in a trash bag that's headed for the dumpster. I wonder what archaeologists a thousand years from now will make of a dirt-laden and ripped cotton t-shirt?

You're not supposed to throw meat or meat scraps into the compost. I buy a whole chicken every couple of weeks and boil it, then debone it for about five days' worth of lunches and dinners plus various soups with a chicken-broth base. What am I supposed to do with the skin, the heart, the neck, the gristle, and the bones? I really cannot bring myself to put them in the trash. I hate the smell of rotting meat in the dumpster I share with nine neighbors.

I've come to the conclusion that I could cremate the meat scraps in the wood stove during the winter, but what to do from May through September? I actually don't mind the critters that frequent my compost pile. The raccoons—being omnivores—will come whether or not there's meat.

And I have to say that I sort of like running across old brown chicken bones in the compost or in the vegetable garden, where they add calcium to the soil. That's about as close to a Buddhist charnel-ground contemplation as I am going to get.

Bones of the dead are scattered, as I have seen at the retreat center I go to in Washington State. The bones of an elk that lay down and died near a trail at the beginning of a retreat four years ago are now covered with grass and moss and spread out over an area bigger than my living room. Those bones that were a creature are now habitat for other living beings.

And the bones that are typing these words onto a page will all be dust in another 40 years.

A BEAUTIFUL ARBOR AGES

SEVERAL YEARS AGO I saw an arbor at the garden center, but before I could commit to buying it, it had disappeared. Oh, darn. I had especially liked the sunrise pattern on the side—a half-circle of wood with thin, wooden slats of sun rays radiating out to the uprights. But the sun had set on the opportunity to buy that beautiful arbor. Sigh.

The following Wednesday morning, I went to writing group, and there stood the arbor. Margot had bought it! I came over a few days later and took measurements and photos. Then I went to the local fencing company and asked the owner to make me such an arbor. Two arbors, in fact, plus four sections of fencing with a sunrise pattern. Eventually the job was completed and installed on summer solstice.

Now I'm in the Wednesday morning writing group again, sitting outdoors at the picnic table and looking at Margot's arbor. A pink rose has clambered over the top, each flower's five simple petals gazing at the morning sun that shines warmly on them this June morning.

I also see that five or eight of the wooden sun rays on either side of the arbor have pulled out of the weather-beaten gray suns, like broken spokes of an old wagon wheel.

The entire arbor stands somewhat off-balance, as if gravity is pulling it toward the east. In ten years this arbor has aged from shiny, smooth, brown to dull, rough gray. Its youthful beauty still imaginable through its cracked age.

We too are of the nature to grow old and gray, our bones thinning, though not visibly but only to be noticed in the triennial bone-density scan. We too begin to favor one leg due to painful knee or hip joints.

Those who love us look deeply and still see us as beautiful. Those new to our acquaintance simply see graying hair and wrinkled faces. They may notice the creping of the skin on our arms, and our general unshapeliness, as if gravity has pulled breasts down to belly and everything else down to hips.

If someone bought this house tomorrow, they'd throw the arbor on the brush pile and burn it to a pile of ashes.

A pile of ash or dust is what our own bodies will turn into. Our physical form, which people loved, returns to the stardust from which it came.

SITTING ON MY DECK IN THE MORNING

Do I wish the robin would sing a different song?
Do I want the woodpecker not to rat-a-tat-tat?
Or the chickadee not to hop into the birdfeeder?
Or do I sigh, "If only the frog hadn't jumped into the pond"?

Do I think the phlox should look different than it does?
Or that the columbine really shouldn't wear that color?
Don't the geraniums know that red and magenta clash?
Or the rhododendrons that their colors are so yesterday?

Sitting on my deck in the early morning,
Nature unfolds moment by moment.

My comparing, judgmental, critical mind comes to rest
in the calmness of what is.
Revealing the uselessness
of any "coulda," "woulda," "shoulda."

Tranquility reflecting the stress
of wanting anything to be different than it is.

I'LL MAKE YOU SPECIAL, IF YOU MAKE ME SPECIAL

HERE'S THE DEAL: I'll make you special if you make me special.

This is the quid pro quo I have with my garden. If I make it a special garden, then it will make me a special gardener. People will (and do) come to stroll around my garden, and then they will think well of me. "Wow. What a great gardener Cheryl is."

We also have this deal with our most-beloved people. "I'll make you special, if you make me special." Marriage partners, family and close friends—we make each other special in return for them making us special. When this unspoken deal fails—for instance, when there is infidelity or talking behind someone's back—a *lot* of suffering, heartache, and stress results.

Sometimes the deal fails in small ways: someone we care about and want to spend time with doesn't want to spend time with us. If the heart doesn't exactly break, it does at least crack.

This is the price of attachment. This is the cost of something that looks like love, but actually has small clinging tendrils wrapping themselves around our hearts. This deal-making opens the heart to some dear ones, but closes it off to others.

In time, I will no longer be able to make my garden special. I will let it go, perhaps piece by piece. Yet, the flowers bloom, not for me alone, but because flowering is what they naturally do.

Relationships drift and tug. Dear friends disappear off the horizon of our life. Strangers arrive. Our heart naturally opens, and we make a new friend. Once upon a time, our hearts were as big as the world. They still are.

LOCAVORE STRESS

I STORE GARLIC, onions, tomatillos, and gladiola bulbs in my unfinished basement. My sweetie built a rack of open shelving that I can simply slide trays into. The open-air concept allows me to see when the onions start to sprout in April.

We have an apartment-sized refrigerator in the basement, and that's where I keep my potato harvest and zip-lock bags full of sun-dried tomatoes. An apartment-sized freezer is stuffed full of green beans, broccoli, and pesto from the garden. Last winter I held more tightly to the locavore concept and actually managed to clean everything out by June. Well, almost everything—I just peeled 50 heads of garlic and stored them in olive oil.

This locavore idea is rooted in the slogan: "Act Locally, Think Globally." By eating locally, we can cut down on all the petroleum needed to transport vegetables from the West Coast to the East.

The fly in the ointment is this: The vegetables at the store are so much more beautiful than the ones in my freezer. And the grocery store has more variety too. Even the local food co-op that sells *only* organic fruits and vegetables (and mostly local) has a more interesting selection than I do in my basement.

I may subscribe to the idea of Voluntary Simplicity, but how does it taste?

A little local chicken broth adds a lot of flavor to green beans. Grated zucchini disappears into blond brownies, heavy on the chocolate chips and walnuts. Put sun-dried tomatoes in the pesto and deplete two storage items at the same time.

Next week: green beans, grated zucchini, some broccoli, and, oh yes, winter squash—*again*. Repeat for 20 weeks.

By April, my sweetie is threatening to throw out the remaining two trays of tomatillos. Quick! Think Mexican. Green chili. Well, the color takes some getting used to, but it actually tastes great. Simmer a pork tenderloin in tomatillos, onions, and garlic for chili verde.

Finally the cellar is bare. I can buy any vegetable I want at the farmers' market. But wait! Late April is the time to pick fiddlehead ferns and wild leeks. Asparagus begins to poke up. I refuse to eat the dandelion green salads I grew up on. Last year's kale resprouts in the garden and has enough tender leaves for two meals a week.

Just when I think I can cut loose from locavoring, the season begins again. Rhubarb, cherry tomatoes, cucumbers. The cornucopia overflows into zip-lock bags, and, now that we're locavoring the sun and producing our own electricity with photovoltaics, it's time to buy a bigger freezer.

THE PERSON I USED TO BE

April showers have come early this year, and the creeks are running near flood stage. Spring runoff, we say. And where does the spring of our life run off to? Where is that young face and lithe body?

The photos of the person I call "me" delude me into thinking that I'm still the person I used to be. In fact, that person is dead now.

Yes, I can remember a lot about her life. Five years of college, living with her boyfriend in Florida. She was a VISTA volunteer in Utah, and I can tell you about all those national parks on the Colorado River Plateau. She fell in love with a Japanese-American and followed him to Hawai'i. I can tell you a lot about Hawai'i. She moved to Vermont to get a master's degree; I live there still.

The events of that young woman's life set in motion a chain of events, and even today I feel the ripples.

The creek is roaring outside the window. In summer it becomes calm and tinkling. Now, in the autumn of my life, the mindstream is littered with the fallen leaves of memories—some clogging little channels and some settling to the bottom to decompose.

The creek flows on. A young middle-aged old life running its course, never able to flow backwards to the person I used to be.

THE MIND

TRANQUILITY

On Wednesday afternoons I teach meditation at an assisted living facility to two old ladies. Ninety-three-year-old Betty wears two hearing aids and still can't hear 91-year old Helen. But Helen can't hear Betty either. I sit between them and boom out meditation instructions.

As usual with beginners, I introduce various objects of meditation because each individual gravitates toward whatever interests her the most—hearing or the breath or sensations of the body. Betty and Helen both find hearing to be most interesting, specifically "the sound of silence."

"Tranquility is my favorite word," says Betty. "Tranquility feels like a forest glade. A still pool, and animals come to drink there."

Betty is a devout Catholic with macular degeneration who watches only animal programs on TV. She's never heard of Ajahn Chah, a Thai Forest Master, who said,

> *Try to be mindful and let things take their natural course. Then your mind will become still in any surroundings, like a clear forest pool. All kinds of wonderful, rare animals will come to drink at the pool, and you will clearly see the nature of all things. You will see many strange and wonderful things come and go, but you will be still. This is the happiness of the Buddha.*

I quiz Betty about the inner quietness she experiences. "Oh yes," she says. "Even when my mind is busy, the quiet is still there."

Two weeks earlier she quoted Shantideva, an eighth-century Indian Buddhist scholar, and she's never heard of him either.

Why worry if you can do something about it? And why worry if you cannot do anything about it?

This is the reason I keep going back to the assisted living facility: I'm learning a lot from Betty.

THE REACTIVE MIND

A THOUGHT ARISES in the mind. Where it comes from, I don't know. All of a sudden there it is, and the remarkable thing is, that I automatically believe it. No matter what that thought tells me, I believe it's true.

Here's an example: "Only one person has signed up for the six-week class I'm teaching, beginning next Tuesday."

The fact of the matter is that one person has signed up. But the place that snags me, catches me, throws me for a loop is the word "only." *Only* one person. *Only* makes me feel lonely. *Only* is already a judgment, an opinion. And I believe it.

Then the mind reacts by comparing. Jack and Claire have 13 people signed up for their Monday night class and another 13 for their Thursday night class.

While this is a fact, I believe that this thought has something to do with me. They have 13 x 2 students; they have 26, I have one.

Can you see where this is going?

The mind believe that word "only." Then it compares. Comparison is a zero-sum game. Greater than? Or less than? In this example, 1 is less than 26.

Therefore I am less than.

Then I believe *that* thought.

Then I feel like shit.

The mind starts to wiggle in all directions. *How can I solve this problem?*

See, I've automatically assumed it's a problem. Now I believe *that* thought.

What if it's an opportunity in disguise? Then I believe *that* thought and begin to brainstorm what I can do with my free Tuesday evenings.

Meanwhile, the original thought is long gone. It has stirred up a little tornado of thoughts and feelings in its wake, each one rippling out its own subsidiary thoughts, beliefs, and comparisons.

And I still believe every single one of these thoughts with all the innocence of a young child believing everything her parents tell her.

WHAT I WOULD HAVE LIKED TO HAVE SAID

I OFTEN REVIEW in my mind what I would have liked to have said, but in fact did not. How could I have said it anyway, since it didn't occur to me until later?

Just last week I was on the Spirituality panel at hospice for the current hospice volunteers-in-training. Four of us on the panel sat just in the right order, as it happened, in front of 20 people.

The Christian talked first, about eternal life. She has been trained in seminary-speak and certainly aspires to be inclusive, to the point where she never uses the word "people," but always refers to "persons." "The persons who are dying. . ." Her voice has that ministerial singsong quality that is used in the pulpit when saving souls but is otherwise never heard in daily life.

Marie—the Baha'i representative—spoke next about several Baha'i rituals and beliefs. The everlasting soul lives on after the death of the body.

Mark, who lives in Massachusetts, participates in the Burial Society at the temple in Greenfield. The Burial Society readies Jewish bodies for burial—women preparing women, men preparing men. Dressing the bodies in white shrouds and placing them in pine boxes, with ceremonies chock-full of rituals.

Last of all I spoke as a Buddhist. "In Buddhism, there is no God, no soul, and no spirit," I said. "There's no self either." At which point, I couldn't imagine why anyone in the room would want to hear anything else I said. "You may be aware of applying your internal brakes," I continued, "because, of course, it feels like we do have a self. And so there must be a soul or a spirit.

"One of the things the Buddha refused to talk about was what happens after death. He just didn't answer the question. His teaching concerning one subject only: Suffering and the end of suffering. He didn't teach what we don't need to know. What happens after death has been discussed for thousands of years, with no one coming to any sure conclusion.

"As far as rituals go," I said, "Buddhism is a recent transplant to this country, so American Buddhism hasn't yet acquired rituals around death." I knew the Tibetan practitioners in the audience would argue with that, because there are a lot of Tibetan rituals.

I wasn't particularly happy with what I said that day. Or with the things I didn't say, like "Remind the dying person of all the good they have done in their lives."

Just a couple of days later, someone mentioned that only 10 percent of what we communicate is in the words we speak, 30 percent is tone of voice, and 60 percent is nonverbal. So maybe it doesn't really matter what I said—or didn't say—to that room full of people. They were hearing my tone and seeing my nonverbal gestures. I was communicating my own comfort with and understanding of the conundrum of death, without saying a word about it.

In the next few days, three people thanked me for what I said.

But that didn't stop me from rewriting the script for what I would have liked to have said. Even if no one remembers the actual words.

MY FAVORITE WORD

My favorite word is *papancha*. It's the Pali word that means "proliferation." Pali is the language that Buddhist texts are written in; it's closely related to Sanskrit.

Papancha, or proliferation, refers to what our minds do all day long—follow one train of thought and then another. We have no idea where these trains of thought are going. Destination: Unknown. We don't really know where the trains come from either. A thought pulls into the station of our mind, and we get on, moving from car to car, thought to thought, till the train we're on slows down, one minute or 15 minutes later. We disembark as though we're sleepwalking, and we board the next train of thought that comes along.

Choo-choo. The next train pulls out of the station. We're so busy talking to ourselves, we don't even notice where we are, how it smells, what it looks like, or how it feels. The Papancha Express sometimes wends through old familiar territory. Sometimes it drags slowly through the night fog of depressing or mean thoughts. Sometimes it zooms along through the flowery meadows of daydreams. We don't even realize that we could just sit at the station and watch the trains come and go. We could even count the cars of separate thoughts. We wouldn't have to buy a ticket. We could sit right here in the present moment, which is where we are anyway.

Then maybe we'll notice that no train of thought is headed to Nirvana. No train has the destination: Wake Island. Rather, these trains of thought are all headed to the Field of Dreams. None of these thoughts will take us where we want to go—to a place of still water, where, if we ourselves are very quiet, all kinds of wild animals will come to drink, and we can sit in awe of wondrous nature.

Give *papancha* a rest. Stop obsessing. Pause from your perseverating. Wrap up your worrying.

Turn away from the trains of thought. Look at the trees, the sunlight on the snow, bronze beech leaves fluttering in a slight breeze. Stop making mountains out of molehills.

Notice the molehills. Yes, it's unpleasant to see those mole tunnels running through your flower bed. Notice the unpleasantness. You don't have to get on the train that runs through the Tunnel of Unpleasantness. Instead, watch that thought crumble until all that remains is a half-second of quiet.

BRAIN WAVES AND BODY WAVES

SINCE A LIGHT wave can also be seen as a particle, and a particle can also be seen as a wave, and since our physical bodies are a collection of billions of particles, then can our bodies also be seen as waves? Waves of light, perhaps, merely passing through space. Now you see it (oh, for, say, an instant of about 80 years); now you don't.

And what would you call a thought? Some sort of brain wave? A momentary blip on the screen—and I do mean momentary—each thought a spark of light, like a shooting star that comes seemingly from nowhere and goes nowhere. A brain wave that looks like *something*—a "particle"—when it's illuminated by our conscious awareness of it. Then gone. Gone. Really gone.

Of course, that doesn't stop us from trying to hang onto that particle of a thought that seems in turn to spark new particles of thoughts—a whole collection of them until we are thinking entire paragraphs to ourselves.

Stop. Stop right there.

Did you notice what I said, what we all say several times every day? We say it so often that we actually believe it.

"We think to ourselves. . ." "I think to myself. . ."

Does that mean there are two of me? I who am thinking, and myself who is aware of the thought? What if, just what if, there is only the thought? A brain wave passing through space. Perhaps brain wave after brain wave lighting up the entire sky like the northern lights.

Where is the "I" who is thinking? As ephemeral as the northern lights, or as a rainbow, simply a phenomenon of light and particles, waves and particles that look like one thing, but, when seen from a different perspective, look completely different. No "I" here. Simply a mask that we try to animate with self. The second we stop, the mask falls mute again.

Oh, God! That can't be!

"I" don't exist? Worse than God being dead, what if I, my I, the I, your I, what if the *self* is dead?

It's unthinkable. I don't want to think this unthinkable thing.

What if my group of particles, my skeleton and muscles, my blood and juices, the air that passes through me are all just particles? The body—composed of solids, liquids, and gases—all just particles in motion? My beautiful body, the one that lies naked on a bed waiting for my lover night after night, my lover who calls me his Odalisque. That body has turned into a phenomenon, too. No longer young, no longer middle-aged. What was firm now sags. What was smooth is now bumpy.

I can now imagine myself as halfway between juicy, ripe flesh and decay. Like an apple held too long in the crisper drawer, going mealy, turning brown in spots, finally fit for nothing but the compost pile. My body, my life, my self composting. Bereft of any identity at all. Identity stolen from me—every moment, it turns out. The name remains the same while the particles are in constant motion. New particles added every second through breathing, drinking, eating. Old particles lost through breathing and elimination or perspiration.

I breathe your air, you breathe mine. Whose air is it? If I tried to reclaim all the particles that have ever been "mine," would I be as big as a town, a county, a state, a country, a continent? I couldn't possibly drag all that physicality around.

Then, in the twinkling of an eye, the flick of the wrist, the turn of a phrase, my particles are also waves. . Simply existing for a moment, then passing. Every moment, the body dies, the mind dies, every moment dies. For a split second we can see the infinity of nothing. Nothingness. No-thing-ness. Because those particle things look like waves. And those wave things look like particles. And nowhere is there an I, a self, a me. No matter how hard I look, nothing is mine, nothing is myself. No breath, no body, no writing, no history, no laugh, no-thing.

The flame of life burns on. Is this moment's flame the same as the previous moment's flame? Not the same, yet not different either. Mind, life, body sparking into existence and then the spark dies into unfindable, unrevivable ash. And if we are dying every instant, then what remains?

Simply life. How can we possibly die?

WHAT I KNOW BEST

WHAT DO I know best? That my mind will forget most of what I think I know. Names first, then the factoids on which I base my opinions. Listening to a 75-year-old friend talk can be like a fill-in-the-blank quiz. "Oh, you know. When what's-his-name said that thing about nuclear power, and why it's bad for ah, ah, ah. . . ."

The opinion survives even though the underlying rationale can no longer be retrieved.

Really, all I can know is what's arriving at my senses this moment—birds are singing, even if I do forget which song belongs to which bird. Traffic is trundling past this house, even if I can't identify the model and year or even the make of each car like I could when I was 15. Peonies and irises are blooming even if my vision is a bit fuzzy. A slight cool breeze is blowing, and the sun that shines upon the roses on the arbor warms my rosy face as well.

SKELETON

I JOINED FREECYCLE.COM a while ago and signed up for the Brattleboro group. The rules for freecycle are pretty simple: Whatever you offer has to be free. And the goal is to recycle the junk that you might otherwise throw away.

When Bill nagged me to do something about the gas grill that had been sitting in our garage since 1998, I finally had to admit that, although grilling seems like a good idea and all my siblings do it frequently, my imagination just didn't extend to grilling tofu a couple of nights a week and tempeh on Sunday evenings.

So I posted the grill on freecycle.com. "To Give Away: Gas grill with cover and grilling utensils."

The next day a red truck pulled in, two hefty guys got out and loaded the black grill into the back of the truck. They looked like the types who would watch a football game on TV, grill up some steaks, and drink some beers. I felt confident the grill was going to a happy home.

I'm in a two-year meditation training program, and the teacher assigned a video for us to watch: *Autopsy*. In the middle of 50 minutes of meeting coroners, medical examiners, and a brain pathologist, I watched them at work, making a Y-incision in the torso, lifting out each organ and weighing it. They took a pair of tree loppers to cut through the rib cage in order to extract the heart and lungs, weigh them, and slice them open with a bread knife.

The word "autopsy" comes from two Greek words: *auto*—as in automatic, autonomic, auto-immune—and *opsis*—as in optical or optometrist. "Auto-opsy" means to see for oneself, which is just what the teacher wanted us to do. See for ourselves what the innards of the body look like.

I did have to pause the video after the brain pathologist made an incision across the scalp, pulled the hair and forehead down to the nose like he was pulling off a Halloween mask, took a circular saw and cut all the way around the skull. As he took two short, fat screwdrivers and pried off the top of the skull, I just had to stop and breathe. Then I resumed playing the video and watched him plop the brain out into his hand. Just like that.

He replaced the skullcap, pulled up the face, made a few stitches in the scalp, and there was a truly brainless, empty-headed corpse.

The following week's assignment was to download a picture of a skeleton, but I thought I might get extra credit if I could find a real skeleton. I posted my request on freecycle.com: "WANTED: skeleton, for studying anatomy class I'm taking." The next day I received an e-mail from the moderator: "Freecycle doesn't allow trading of illegal items. We think skeletons are illegal."

Sigh. I was stymied. Then the next assignment arrived in the mail—a DVD entitled *Cemetery Contemplations*, a daily video log of a decomposing body in a tropical country. Soon there was nothing left but a skeleton.

I had to race through this assignment, because we were leaving for England the next day. As it turned out, at my month-long retreat in England, the meditation center had just received the gift of a skeleton. There it sat, cross-legged, in meditation pose, surrounded by giant split-leaf philodendrons. Every time I did walking meditation in that room, I placed myself as close to the skeleton as possible, walking toward it and becoming intimate with the details of its bones.

Skeletons may be "illegal," but we all have them. To be able to see one "in real life" and study it is a great gift. By looking at a skeleton we do our own auto-opsy — we see with our own eyes — the frame of the vehicle that carries us around, the skeleton that will one day be recycled into Mother Earth.

DARKNESS

THE HOUSE
ON THE MOORS

THE HOUSE ON the moors settles toward sleep, but I open the big blue door around which the damp chill of the evening breathes in. I can feel the temperature indoors dropping around me as I put on my shoes, and zip up my polar fleece jacket, and zip up my Gore-Tex shell, and pull on my hat and gloves.

I walk out the ancient big blue door into darkness. The pockets of my shell are loaded: a flashlight here, a compact umbrella there, a small clock that, when I press a tiny button, lights up the time. But I want none of these aids tonight as I step into darkness and close the door to the manor house behind me.

I step gingerly ahead, knowing that, although I can't see it, the ground is paved here and the pavement continues all the way down the driveway. I hear church bells ringing the hour in Denbury, a mile away through the sheep pastures. Nine o'clock and crystalline stars shimmer above. The Big Dipper twinkles directly overhead. I walk slowly down the black driveway, thankful now for the hedge border that offers some protection from the slight breeze. With each slow step, I offer a prayer of kindness toward a different friend.

I walk as far as the spreading oak, where the darkness becomes darker. I turn and pace slowly up the drive. Now I can see the manor house with its additions spread like wings on both sides. Three lighted windows on the second floor to the north, curtains drawn in hopes of cutting down the draft. Two lighted windows on the ground floor to the right, light spilling out and soaked up immediately by the night.

Close to the house, I turn and walk away again. I know that a hill rises in front of me, a mile away. Ancient people lived there, but all that remains is a 2,500-year-old hill fort and a thousand-year-old burial cairn.

My eyes are now accustomed to the dark, which seems blue-black. I am breathing chilled air, my chin bent into my muffling scarf. My body longs for warmth, so I walk into the big house and close the blue door behind me. Taking off my shoes, I pull on slippers and glide quietly over 400-year-old paving stones worn smooth by thousands of feet.

Coats hung up on a peg, I climb two flights of stairs to my room, where I exchange my heavy pair of polar fleece pants for polar fleece leggings, and my polar fleece top for a light merino wool sweater. Back home, this outfit would be day clothes, but here they are my night clothes, as I snuggle into a single bed and pull the duvet over my head. Darkness.

THE NAME OF THE DARK

FIREFLIES GLOW IN the summer night, providing a momentary incandescence. I park a flashlight between us in the hammock and arrange a fleece coverlet to warm us in the coolness of the June evening. We look for the moon that rose late tonight and is still climbing its way up the eastern sky behind us. We lie awake and look for stars whose names we've already forgotten dozens of times. Rigel, Betelgeuse, Sirius, we guess, but have no confidence. After all, a star is a star whether or not it has a name. Calling it by a name is really just to make ourselves feel good about ourselves.

"Yes. That one is definitely Rigel," we say, as if it were true. As if the name had anything to do with anything.

Really, we all just agree to call that brightest star in the constellation of Orion, "Rigel." The name has nothing to do with the star itself.

Just like my parents decided to name me Cheryl. All my life I've answered to that word, as if it were really me. As if there were some Cheryl-ness about me. Actually, it's just that everyone has agreed to call me "Cheryl." When I was born, I was a nameless body. When I die, I will be a nameless body again—a body infirm with age or sickness. A body devoid of personality or person-ness. This body ages and decays and isn't actually the same from day to day.

Yet people persist in calling me "Cheryl," as if I were that four-year-old with eczema, the 12-year-old with asthma so severe she couldn't breathe. The 22-year-old who kissed her boyfriend and learned about sex between tiger-striped sheets. The 30-year-old who had severe bouts of night-thinking about how inadequate she was. The 45-year-old who spooned into her lover and spoke gently to the night. Now that body has reached retirement age, and yet it goes out several nights a week—to write, to meditate, to volunteer, to eat with friends at potlucks. Eventually, she thinks, she will slow down.

But for now, she gazes at the night sky and squeezes the hand of the body lying next to her.

TORNADO

*In memory of
my Great-Aunt Mary Hawks Hawkins
and the day she flew.*

TORNADO SEASON

Mary

Mary glanced at her gold Timex. 11:55. She was ready for lunch. Even though Sears would close at noon, she'd have to spend another half an hour or so cashing out. On Wednesdays, all the businesses in Greenfield closed at noon for the rest of the day, even the bank. In exchange, they were all open on Saturday mornings, even the bank, when the farmers came to town.

She glanced out over the mezzanine railing to see how many customers were still in the store. She had time to run another column of numbers. Then she counted the till, made out the deposit slip, and zipped it all into the green canvas bag. She was the last employee out of the store, and she made sure the door was locked behind her. She walked the half block to the Greenfield Banking Company and placed the bag in the night depository slot. Unconsciously, she breathed a sigh of relief. She quickened her step past Danner Brothers' five- and ten-cent store, turned the corner, walked past Sears and into the parking lot.

As she got into her car she was thinking about tomorrow evening's Maundy Thursday service at which the Lord's Supper would be served. She wondered how Jesus had felt during the day of His last supper. How had He felt before the Last Supper, before He and His disciples went up to the Garden of Gethsemane? How had He felt during the day? Did the foreknowledge that His mortal end was near come to Him all of a sudden? Did God speak directly to Him? Or did the knowing creep over His awareness until He was somehow sure?

She was still mulling these ideas over when she pulled up beside the Trinity Park United Methodist Church five minutes later. Using her key to let herself into the office, she picked up a folder full of bills, a checkbook, and a journal. Now, finally, she could go home.

Without thinking, she found herself headed south on State Street; people around here simply called it 9. Her red Buick crossed Main Street, or 40, as most people called it. She'd always liked its old name. The National Road. That's what her parents had called it, back when roads had names instead of numbers. She had always lived about a mile south of the National Road. Spending her life that close to a national landmark gave her a sense of place, located her in space, in a very specific space. Greenfield, Indiana. The National Road ran through the middle of Greenfield and connected Washington, D.C., to San Francisco, California. She'd never been to either end of the National Road. She'd always been right here in the middle: Indiana called itself the "Crossroads of America." Living at the so-called crossroads she saw a lot of trucks and cars, and trains for that matter, all headed somewhere else. She'd like to go, too. Go as far as she could.

Two blocks south of the National Road her foot touched the brake lightly as she looked quickly left and right down the double set of tracks of the Pennsylvania Railroad. She crossed these tracks twice a day every day of her life—once on the way to work and again on the way home. She'd been working for Sears for nearly 35 years, and before that, Broadway Lumber for ten years. When she was a girl, she'd crossed the railroad tracks on her way to school and again on her way home. She looked right again and could see the closed-up building of the Greenfield Ice Cream Company, a block to the west.

A slight tingle was all that remained of the time when she was 12. One summer day, she and her best friend Myrtle had somehow gotten hold of a dime. They headed straight to the Greenfield Ice Cream Company to get themselves cones. She'd probably had strawberry; she'd always liked strawberry. As they sat there between the building and the railroad tracks, they'd hatched a plan. Daring each other, Myrtle had laid a penny on the rail just before the afternoon train came rushing through. They'd stood close, keeping one eye on the penny to watch if they could see where it flipped to, but mostly they stood awed by the size and speed of the train, rushing so close by them. So tall, so powerful, so noisy. They couldn't stand the vertigo, the combination of noise and wind and shaking; they had thrown themselves on the ground just five feet away from the tracks, which had been both better and worse. Better because that fear of falling into the train's path was gone, but worse because now they could feel the rumble of the train all up and down and through their young, skinny bodies.

When the train finally whooshed all the way past them, they waved at the man in the caboose and then they laughed hard. Standing up felt like standing in someone else's body. They laughed some more. They hunted for the penny and finally found it. "Flatter than a flitter," Myrtle said. And they laughed again.

More recent than the tingle of that faint 50-year-old memory was the recollection of people killed when trying to cross these very tracks. Farm trucks that stalled, or teenagers on a lark racing the train and losing, or. . . She didn't totally trust the red flashing lights and the black-and-white-striped arm that guarded the crossing. Now the lights gazed blankly with their hooded eyes, and the crossing arm pointed its long finger to the gray, cloudy sky. Still, she looked both ways and looked both ways again as her car rumbled over that double set of tracks.

She sighed. Geraniums. Red, of course. She liked red. This year she'd buy red geraniums. She drove past the entrance to Park Cemetery where John was buried. Even though it was only April 3 she was already thinking about what to put on the grave. Two more months until Memorial Day. Then she'd set out a couple of geraniums at their headstones. His stone had both dates filled in: John Hawkins, July 14, 1903–June 16, 1966. Her matching stone just told her name and birth date: Mary E. Hawkins, May 17, 1912.

Next month she'd turn 62. Sixty-two! How could she be that old? She only had a few gray hairs. The cute dimples she used to have had turned into deep creases in her cheeks. She still felt young, too young to retire. She could retire, she considered for the hundredth time, but she hadn't signed up for Social Security yet. She figured she'd wait till 65. Once more she weighed the pros and cons of retiring and mentally reviewed her widow's financial picture.

Automatically she turned east on 100 South. As she neared home her thoughts turned to the flower beds. Well, they were hers, they'd been hers for years now, but she still thought of them as Annie's. John's mother's flower beds. Annie had been gone twelve years. John and Mary had moved into her house after Annie had become senile and gone to live with John's older sister, Burl. Annie's yellow climbing rose still trailed all over the back fence. The peonies still grew alongside the driveway, along with the hydrangeas that had stood beside the old homestead that had burned down in 1932. Still, the flowers came back year after year. The peonies were just now spreading their red fingertips out of the dark Hoosier dirt as if reaching for the sky.

She flicked on the windshield wipers. No gardening this afternoon. She pulled into her driveway, lined on the east side with a row of twisted, gray catalpa trees. She loved the big clusters of white, orchid-looking, oh-so-sweet-smelling catalpa blossoms, but she sure did hate to clean up those long brown bean-pods they produced in the fall. She was just listening to the one o'clock news on the car radio. Straight ahead she could see the barn, which needed a coat of paint. Since John had died, and she'd sold his beloved cows, she rented out the farmland to her neighbor, Cecil Peacock. He stored hay in the barn for his cattle, but that's about all the use that old barn ever got nowadays.

She turned left into the one-car garage. Just before she turned off the ignition she heard the weather report that followed the one o'clock news. Thunderstorms. And tornado warnings.

She dashed up the narrow sidewalk that led to the back door of the little bungalow. She stepped into the open-air back porch that had been John's bedroom after he'd gotten TB while working with the cattle at Eli Lily and Company in Greenfield. That's how they treated tuberculosis back then. No workman's compensation, just lots of fresh air. The TB had settled in John's knees. He'd been too proud to use crutches, so he'd hobbled on two canes for the rest of his life. He'd been gone for eight years now. She sighed and opened the storm door and the door that led into the kitchen.

She hung up her coat, put the church's bookkeeping work on the kitchen table, and made herself some tomato soup and a grilled-cheese sandwich. After lunch, she walked through the little living room that still smelled of old-lady lavender, even though Annie had been gone for all these years. Mary walked into the bedroom that was just big enough for a double bed and a chest of drawers. She kicked off her shoes and lay down and covered herself with a red, coral, and brown afghan she'd crocheted, and she closed her eyes.

Half an hour later, Mary sat at the kitchen table, concentrating on the checkbook and the journal that lay open before her. She'd been church treasurer for how long? It took a few hours each week to pay the bills and balance the books, but she liked the volunteer work. She'd always been good with numbers, and she'd been a member of this church, well, ever since she skipped the fifth grade and went directly into sixth. She reconciled the March bank statement. Then she wrote this week's checks.

Outside the old windmill churned. They hadn't needed it since rural electrification came through in 1939. Now it squeaked and clattered noisily. The bare lilac bushes beat against the edge of the living room window.

She was just figuring out the church's quarterly withholding taxes that were due next week. She had added the numbers from the payroll cards, but the total didn't match the percentage of gross payroll. She was just double-checking her work, so she took no notice of the first rumble. The railroad was a mile away, but sometimes she could hear the trains quite clearly if the wind was right. Noise traveled easily over open corn and soybean fields. Or maybe it was thunder. She glanced at her watch — 3:00. It seemed kind of dark in the kitchen.

She heard hail pelting the windows. She stood up, stretched her back, and looked out the kitchen window. Her jaw opened a fraction of an inch, and time seemed to move like sorghum molasses.

Mary saw the barn go flying by the house in thousands of pieces, then the milk house lifted off its foundation and disappeared. She threw herself down on the floor under the kitchen table. The linoleum rippled underneath her. The floorboards underneath the linoleum begin to jump and tug and pull. The noise was deafening.

"Oh, Jesus, help me!" she prayed, her face as close to the earth as it was possible to be and still be in a house. Had she lost her vision or was it really this dark? Dark as night. She thought of John. She thought of her mother, who had died only four years ago, and of her long-dead father. She thought of her sisters, Margaret and Frances. She thought of Annie who had spent her 30-year widowhood in this little one-bedroom bungalow.

"Oh, Lord, bless all of them. Help me to get through this. I need your help, O Jesus."

She heard the storm door rattling hard in its frame. She tried to hunker down even more but failed. She didn't hear glass shattering, but she felt a hundred pin pricks hit her body. She felt a trainload of wind. So this was it? This was how it happened? It seemed as if all the air had been sucked out of the house. She couldn't breathe. "Oh God!" she prayed.

She didn't even feel her body hurtling through space.

Paul

Being indoors and listening to all that yammering made him feel itchy, so he'd made his escape soon after he and his young family had arrived at his in-laws' house. While his mother-in-law, Anne, talked to his pregnant wife, Teresa, and played with his almost-three-year-old daughter, Tracy, he'd simply disappeared. Paul headed toward the low one-room log cabin he'd built for himself.

He walked across an open field to the strip of woods along Sugar Creek. He liked walking in the woods, always had. He wished he had lived back in the days when Indiana was all woods, before the trees were cleared and the land was broken into 80-acre farms. Right now he was keeping his eyes open for sponge mushrooms, or morels as some people called them.

Paul had walked here a dozen times in the past three weeks, ever since the tornado had come through, trying to understand the destruction. Not too much farther on, the woods took on a peculiar look as if houses had been held aloft and then shaken like pepper over a narrow strip of land. There were the usual broken branches that bespoke the aftermath of a gusty, lusty Midwestern thunderstorm, but no downed or uprooted trees. He guessed that the tornado had hopped right here, its single foot in midair before landing hard again somewhere farther north. He saw a tin roof wrapped into a tree top. Then twenty yards farther on, the little woods returned to its woodland business, walnut trees and ash trees heavy with buds, the honeysuckles already showing miniature spring-green leaves.

Every time he'd walked here recently he'd noticed something new, some postscript of that phenomenal day. When he was a kid, he'd heard tornado stories of straw impaling telephone poles, and now he saw it for himself. A shaft of unbroken wheat straw pierced a tree. He touched it gingerly and tugged it to see if it would come out clean and whole, but it just crumpled between his fingers. A tangle of wire fencing. A ripped sweater. A wadded up blanket. In the midst of a potpourri of wood fragments, a whole board unaccountably untouched. All manner of household goods strewn here and there. Paper—an amazing amount of paper trash littered the earth beneath the trees. Plastic bags or shreds of plastic sat among spring beauties or waved like flags in the treetops. Jack-in-the-pulpits bent out from under a remnant of taupe carpeting. Occasional shards of china or glass reflecting today's sunlight lay among Dutchmen's breeches. A plastic tumbler sat on a log as if someone were just coming back for it.

 He took another step. A letter caught his eye. He bent down for a closer look: Mary Hawkins, Rural Route 1, Greenfield, Indiana 46140. His hand reached out to pick it up. Aunt Mary! A letter to Aunt Mary! She lived ten, eleven, no, twelve miles away from here. Paul shook his head and sat down on the log beside the plastic tumbler. He started thinking about Great-Aunt Mary and the tornado.

An hour after the tornado had passed, the sun was shining. A few small, white, fluffy clouds hung in the clear blue sky. Paul hadn't even known that a tornado had rampaged through the countryside three miles east of his house trailer. He'd just come home from work, and Teresa had just returned from her mother's, where she'd left little Tracy. Teresa told him that a tornado had come really close to her mother's house.

The young couple hopped in the car and turned on the radio, hoping to hear tornado news. They drove east to find the twister's route. In order to follow it, they kept zigzagging south, then west, then south on Hancock County's gravel roads. They gaped at the amazing, weird and fascinating results of wind that had blown more than a hundred miles an hour.

All of a sudden Paul saw his parents' car up ahead, sitting in a driveway. What the heck were they doing here? And then he realized where he was: This was Aunt Mary's driveway, but where was her house? He was quite good at navigating, so he was pretty sure of where he was, but the disappearance of the house made him think for a minute that he really was the stupid kid he'd been in school. "Wha-a-a?" he muttered aloud. He pulled up beside the blue Chevy Caprice with a white vinyl roof.

All the catalpa trees beside the driveway looked like they'd been through a war. Three were just jagged snags. Two had been totally uprooted. The others had had all their little branches blown off, and only the thickest parts of their skeletons remained. Aunt Mary's red Buick sat beyond them. Didn't she used to have a garage? Dead cows lying on their sides with their eyes wide open cluttered the nearby field. Not the field they usually pastured in, but the field across the road.

"Where's Aunt Mary?" Paul asked his mother. Aunt Mary was really her aunt.

"They've taken her away. Oh my God. . ."

The wetness glinting in his mother's eyes made him feel uncomfortable and out of place, so he was thankful when his dad called to him, "Paul! See that cow over there?"

One white-faced Hereford, still alive, had a two-by-four driven through her like a giant's arrow. She was lying on the ground and panting hard.

His dad said, "She's pregnant and about to calve. Reach in there and help her." Reach into that black, bloody, oozing hole. Paul didn't consider disobeying. He got down on his knees.

"Stick your arm in there and feel the legs and pull it out," his dad ordered.

Paul set his jaw and reached into that slimy, dark, cold pulp and grabbed something firm. Seeking to get a better grip, he sat down on the ground and placed his feet against the cow's auburn backside and tugged and pulled. Finally, about ten minutes later, although it seemed like an hour, using all of his strength he yanked out a calf that wobbled but stood her ground.

The Neighbors

The stormy afternoon precluded Cecil Peacock from being out in his equipment shed putting a new fanbelt on his tractor, so he sat in his living room catching up on the *Greenfield Reporter*. He was just reading an article in Monday's paper, "Few Tornadoes Reported This Year." March was generally the big tornado month in Indiana, he read, but this year tornadoes had tracked well south of the Hoosier state. "April may be a bigger month for thunderstorms." Cecil figured they probably had that one right.

He heard hail hitting the windows, so he stood up and watched the weather from his living room window, which faced west. He could see Mary Hawkins' farm from here—the little house, the barn, the milk house, and the garage. Ever since John had died, he'd rented the land from Mary and farmed it. Sometimes he kept a few of his farm implements down there in John's barn.

Then he saw it. A black funnel cloud, dancing over there in the southwest. He called excitedly to his wife and to the carpenters, Darryl and Tom, who were there doing some remodeling. Standing in a row together, they all saw the tornado hit Mary's barn and then her house. They stood rooted to the floor for a moment, waiting to see if the funnel would turn toward them next, but it kept its half-mile distance.

As soon as it disappeared behind some woods to the north, Cecil shouldered on a navy blue nylon windbreaker and grabbed a feed cap that said "DeKalb" on an ear of corn with two wings. While his wife tied her pink chiffon scarf under her chin, he stooped to tie up his clodhoppers. The Peacocks ran directly out to his red Ford pickup truck and climbed in. He backed out of the driveway and sped south for half a mile, then turned west.

As soon as Mr. and Mrs. Peacock barreled out of the house, Darryl and his buddy Tom looked at each other. All their Hoosier lives they'd heard about tornadoes, but they'd never actually seen one. They'd grown up with tornado warnings, but nothing had ever happened. Until now. They were not going to be left out of this rare excitement. They rushed out of the house and across the cornfields, almost running, and cut kitty-corner across the fields along the shortest route to the place where the neighbor's house had been just five minutes earlier. As they climbed over the fences between fields they shook their heads in disbelief at the trash stuck to the fence like multi-colored tumbleweeds.

Meanwhile, Cecil and his wife were staring at Mary's house, if it could still be called that. The northwest corner stood alone. It was only three feet tall. The cement steps leading to the front door, the steps nobody ever used, had been turned perpendicularly to the house. A green sofa lay on its back in the front yard. Two chairs had been thrown nearby. Cecil gazed into the exposed cellar, now filled with tangled and smashed ductwork. The furnace lay at an on its side. Had Mary taken shelter in her basement, like the tornado advisory recommended? He wasn't sure he wanted to look under all that tortured metal. Still, he thought he should go into the cellar hole, but he hesitated.

Meanwhile the carpenters stared at the dead cows with their legs splayed grotesquely sideways, at balled-up fencing and broken lumber, at cans of food all bent and punctured, at paper scattered everywhere. A dented washing machine stood upside down on its top back corner. And then they saw her.

A body. A body covered with little gashes. Some blood smeared, but not really a lot of blood. Hail was melting on the ground beside her. Her white blouse was shredded, showing her bare shoulder. Her bra was hanging loose under the ravelings that used to be a slip. Her muddy beige skirt hung in strips with pieces missing. She was barefoot.

Her eyes opened. Darryl yelled for Cecil, whom he could see standing at the ruins of a house.

Cecil turned and looked north at the hollering, waving carpenters. "Mother," he said to his wife, "better go get some blankets." Then he ran as fast as he could toward the wildly gesturing men.

As he came hurrying toward them, Tom asked Darryl, "Should we move her?"

Darryl shrugged as he knelt down on the earth. "Maybe she's got some broken bones." He didn't really want to touch her, but he wanted to get a closer look.

He glanced up to see if Cecil was on his way; maybe Cecil would know what to do. But Cecil was standing in the road waving his arms like a crazy man.

The Ambulance

At 3:10 a call came in to the Civil Defense. A tornado had hit Stringtown, three miles east of Greenfield on the National Road. Within five minutes an ambulance flashed its way into Stringtown and pulled up next to the newly built Stringtown Nazarene Church. Its roof was gone. Completely gone. The limestone walls still stood; apparently this church had been built upon a rock, all right. From the vantage point of the emergency volunteers in their vehicle on the highway, the tops of the interior walls could be seen, as if prayers might ascend to heaven faster with no interference between the one who prayed and her God.

The ambulance couldn't enter the parking lot because the church bus was in the way, lying on its top. Three men stood near it talking to each other. The rescue workers hurried out of the ambulance and stepped around the bus's back door, which lay cast off on the pavement. One of the three men told his story.

"It was raining and then hailing so hard, I pulled off the highway and into the church parking lot right next to the bus. I'd only been sitting there a minute or two before the bus raised up into the air, jumped over my car, and landed there." He pointed to the upside-down, light blue school bus that had "Stringtown Church of the Nazarene" lettered on its side.

"I thought I was a goner," he said.

The rescuers asked about injuries. A man in overalls said, "I think that tornado must'a lifted off the ground right about here."

The rescue workers scampered back to the ambulance. "I think we should go south here on 500 East," one of them told the driver. "Maybe we'll find something."

"Yeah," said the driver. "According to the radio, things is really bad down in Fountaintown." He drove the ambulance across the National Road south onto the gravel county road named 500 East. The ambulance lights were still flashing even though he could safely travel no more than 40 miles an hour.

The would-be rescuers scanned the unplowed fields. When they got to the next crossroad, they turned west, headed back toward Greenfield just a mile south of the National Road. They looked for signs that they were intersecting the tornado's path again. What they saw five hundred yards in front of them was a man in a green feed cap waving his arms wildly.

Mary

She heard the men's voices coming toward her. She wanted to say, "Hey, I need some help." But she couldn't raise her arm. Words refused to come out of her mouth. She couldn't even turn her head to look for the men who belonged to the voices. *Where the heck was she?* she wondered. Then she saw the two men standing over her, looking down at her and talking excitedly. She was lying on something cold. In fact, she felt cold all over. What was she wearing anyway?

Now the men bent down. She struggled to recognize them, to say something, but she couldn't. Her brain seemed to be working very slowly. She heard the loudness and the excitement in their voices.

Then a man in white was standing over her, talking loudly to her. "Mary! Can you hear me?"

She felt pressure on her wrist, and her whole arm felt like it was being sawed. She saw Cecil standing behind the man in white, and she wanted to say, "What's going on here, Cecil?" but she couldn't. She could see the worried look on his face, but she was actually feeling quite calm and even light.

"Mary! Stay with me!" the man in white commanded.

She felt something tighten around her upper arm. It hurt like the dickens wherever he touched her. She wished he'd stop it. Then her arm got really tight, and she wanted to groan with the pain.

"Mary! Stay with me!"

She was starting to get irritated at this guy. She just wanted to close her eyes and take a little nap, and he kept shouting at her. She didn't even understand when he told another man dressed just like him, "I'm not getting anything here." She just barely noticed that she was being lifted and carried on something flat. They bumped her into something, and then she felt a pinprick in her arm. It was so nice and warm in here. Her eyes closed.

May 1975

"Oh, honey," Mary laughed to her great-niece, "I just can't remember a *thing* about being in that tornado. The doctors said that the pressure in it was so great that I must have just blacked out. All I remember is that when I saw the barn fly past, I just laid down under the kitchen table and prayed."

The young woman looked around the clean double-wide that sat on the same location as the old house. A small collection of five ceramic and porcelain cats sat on the shelf of an étagère.

"But wouldn't you have been safer in the cellar?" she asked.

"Oh, no, honey," she said. "I don't think so. They was such a tangle down there that I'd a-been thrown against them metal pipes and then. . . ." She shrugged and opened her hands to the heavens. "Them tornadoes hop and skip, they say. And right at the house it must-a nearly drilled itself into the ground, if such a thing was possible.

"After it threw me over there in the cornfield," she said, motioning across the road, "I heard those two men walking across the field, but I just couldn't move a muscle. I had hundreds of little cuts from swirling around up there with all my china and such. When they got me to the hospital, they had to cut off my clothes. They was so shredded. That's when they noticed my watch was still ticking." She held out her left wrist to show her great-niece her small gold watch. "It's a Timex." She laughed. "You know what they say."

"Anyway, my arms was shredded too. They looked just like raw meat. The doctors just laid me on one of them hospital beds in my birthday suit. They wanted the air to get at all those cuts so they'd heal. You'd think," she said confidentially, "that my body had enough air strike it already to last a lifetime." She laughed again.

"But my lifetime wasn't over yet. Greenfield Hospital had never had a tornado survivor before, so plenty o' people come in to take a look at me. I just laid there on that hospital bed with a sheet over me. These men'd come in, lift up the sheet, take a look, and cover me up again. I didn't say anything, and they didn't say anything." She smiled.

"I turned pert near every color o' the rainbow. The second week in the hospital I was black and blue and the next week green and yellow from all them bruises. I'm telling you. I was *sore*."

"Six weeks I was in the hospital. Then I stayed with my sister, Frances, till this was finished." She waved her hand vaguely around the living room of the double-wide. "I tell you, this has been quite a year." She shook her head slowly back and forth.

"Did you know that Sears is moving out of Greenfield? Closing its doors. Guess I'll have to see if they'll transfer me over to Indianapolis, so's I can work till I turn 65."

From the end table beside her chair she picked up a box that looked like a 10-by-14-inch picture frame except that it was three inches deep. "I call this my shadow box," she said. "This is everything that's left from the tornado." She opened the lid and took things out one by one and handed them to her great-niece. "Here's one of John's bronzed baby shoes."

She took out two photos. One was of her and John sometime early in their marriage, before he needed two canes to walk.

"Here's the letters that your brother Paul found in the woods up by his log cabin. Just bills," she confided.

One by one she displayed what remained of her former life.

"Here's something I just added a couple of weeks ago. She picked up a thick splinter of wood about an inch and a half long. "Last month, my back hurt something terrible. I kept asking Frances to look at it for me, but she couldn't see anything. Finally one night when I was in bed, I reached around there and felt this. That darn splinter finally worked its way out." She shook her head. "Don't that beat all?

"Your mom and your Aunt Jenny went out and walked the fields the next day after the tornado. They found some of my towels and a quilt I had pieced. Your mom said she had to wash that quilt three times before all the mud come out of it.

"Here. Take a look at this picture." She handed her niece a black and white photo. "That's the northwest corner of the barn. After it was all over, that rattan chair was still sitting in the corner of the barn. And can you believe it? Them money plants I hung up there to dry in September was still hanging there, just as pretty as you please, after the tornado.

"Well, let's go out and look at the flower beds," said Mary. "I think those peonies are coming up."

www.ingramcontent.com/pod-product-compliance
Lightning Source LLC
Chambersburg PA
CBHW072337300426
44109CB00042B/1658